Life Should Be
Simple and Easy
If You're Doing It Hard,
You're Doing It Wrong

by
Dr. Conrad Aquino, M.D.
and Bryson Miller

Stress Free Initiative, Inc.
Clarksburg, MD

Copyright © 2017
by Dr. Conrad Aquino, MD and Bryson Miller

The authors of this book do not dispense medical advice or prescribe the use of any technique as a form of treatment for physical, emotional, or medical problems without the advice of a physician, either directly or indirectly. The intent of the authors is only to offer information of a general nature to help you in your quest for emotional and spiritual well-being. In the event you use any of the information in this book for yourself, which is your constitutional right, the authors, and the publisher assume no responsibility for your actions.

First Edition

ISBN 978-1535449441

stress**free**initiative**.org**

Dedicated to

Christine

and the kids.

Great appreciation to

Julio Giulietti,

for showing the way.

Table of Contents

Weekly Planner

1 Preface

Introduction

Week 1 **7**

Getting Ready

33 Week 2

The Past Determines Today

Week 3 **55**

What is Real?

83 Week 4

The Higher Power

Week 5 **105**

Today Does Not Rely on the Past

127 Week 6

Life Should Be Simple and Easy

Nonprofit **143**

Works Cited **147**

About the Authors **151**

Preface

Introduction

I still remember that day as if it were yesterday. It was a morning in spring of 2008. The heat of the sun, as it hit me, stirred me from my bed. I'd already started my regular morning routine when I noticed something different. Everything felt so simple and easy. The heaviness, the sensation of being dragged down, was gone. I could tell that, from that day onward, my life would never be the same."

This is how one of the authors, Conrad, recalls what we call the De Novo event. It's an awakening to a new life, and it feels like a light bulb came on over your head.

"To this day, I wake up every morning the same, exact way. And each morning, I still feel amazed at this life that I live. It's a gift, no doubt. I've been graced by the powers that be, and I cannot imagine any other life but this. This life is just too good to miss out on. So, I said to myself, as I saw other people suffering through life, it would be unfair for the Higher Power to only select a chosen few. People can't be meant to live and die and not see life in this way. So, with the help of a friend who has received the same gift, we wrote this book."

Stress knows no boundaries, and the epidemic of disappointment and stress reaches everyone. It was no different for the authors.

Dr. Conrad Aquino sought a career in healthcare. He worked as a physician for several years. At the time of publication, he's Assistant Director of Professional Services for one of the fastest growing healthcare companies in the Washington DC area. He faced many challenges growing up, which continued throughout medical school. At a young age, he experienced a stress-related heart attack, and later, shortly after marriage, chose to uproot himself from his hometown and family to pursue a better life. Unfortunately, life became even more stressful for this doctor, but several anxiety attacks later, Conrad experienced his De Novo event in March of 2008 and has been stress-free ever since.

Bryson Miller served as an Aerospace Physiologist in the U.S. Air Force and has a second-degree black belt in kung fu. He joined the military to sustain a relationship and to build a better life, but found that it caused a strain over time. After serving the military, he returned home to be in the comfort of family and friends, unknowing of the challenges that laid waiting: his father was diagnosed with brain cancer, and several of his friends having tragic, untimely deaths. Pressing forward, he continued to try to have a serious relationship, only to find himself in a constant cycle of love and loss. Stress continued to build and pushed him into despair, but Bryson experienced his De Novo event in October of 2010 and has been stress-free ever since.

Life after the De Novo event is wonderfully unique, and thus, so is this book. As you read on, you'll discover that it's very different from other self-help books you've picked up. Let me tell you upfront that this book isn't for everyone. It's not a temporary fix for your stressful life, and its message may even evade you. But, if you are able to comprehend the ideas it explains, and if you can apply their meaning, this will be the last self-help book you'll ever need.

What this book offers is a concept. It's a concept that will survive every trial you'll encounter, every decision you'll make, every step you'll take in life. This book will make you responsible for your life. When you're able to understand the concept that's core to this book, you'll have the answer to the age-old question, "What is the meaning of life?"

> *Two men looked out from prison bars; one saw the mud, the other saw stars.*
> – Dale Carnegie, *How to Stop Worrying and Start Living*

This book won't tell you to keep looking up to the stars. This book will show you the way out of prison.

Instructions on How to Read and Process

This book isn't intended to be read from front to back in one sitting. Instead of chapters, we have 'weeks', and this is for a reason – this is the minimum amount of time it should take to properly consider each section. Often, one week may not be enough to properly digest an entire section. When this is the case, take your time; let each section gel in you, digesting its concepts carefully. It's best that you understand one week before proceeding to the next, because each new concept will build on the mental work that has gone before. You may already be familiar with certain concepts, but don't skip past them or even rush your reading. We believe that going through the book in the right manner is the best way to the path of living a life that's simple and easy.

Know, however, that understanding these concepts won't be enough; you have to come to terms with them. You shouldn't just take them into your mind, but take them into your heart. You may need to read a week more than once to fully understand it and grasp its full meaning. It may take you months or even years to finish this book, but I assure you, it'll be worth it.

The only way to understand the simple lessons of life is to experience them, but even then, learning doesn't happen overnight. Because of this, each week will end with opportunities to pause, and experience, and experiment, and live. There'll even be exercises to start you off. Know that these pauses are just as important as the text. You'll also find a few pages that you can use as you wish. You can take down notes, write what you feel about some ideas, or maybe just try to scribble away your stress. I believe it may be useful to some of you.

Godspeed on your journey.

Week 1

Getting Ready

This Week's Content

Everyone wants a better life. Or... do they? In real life, that statement isn't entirely accurate. The truth is that everyone thinks they want a better life, but no one has the heart to take a step towards it. I know you've picked up this book as a means towards the better life you seek; you've made several steps in order to change your life for the better, yet you've ended up here. Book in hand, mind focused and eyes attentive, you're hoping that this will be the key to unlocking that life of ease and simplicity.

Unfortunately, it's not so easy. The title of this book may say that life should be simple and easy, but the journey to get there is an entirely different story. The path to achieving this life is a challenge on its own. It's difficult, it's arduous, it's grueling, but be assured that if you meet this challenge, everything else will be simple and easy.

Living the simple and easy life is an amazing feeling. Thoughts of it flash in and out of your mind throughout your daily routine. It flutters into your mind during yoga, it catches your attention while riding the bus, and it nestles in your heart even while you're asleep. You know that no other concept or word has rung clearer bells for you than this. You feel empty without it. You feel alone in a world full of people.

Believe it or not, where you are right now is familiar to many, many people. You may be the average office worker who gets up early in the morning, sits in traffic, and gets to the office, never missing a day. You may be the single mom trying to keep two jobs to make ends meet. You may be the abused. You may be the dumped. You may be the jobless, the homeless, or the hopeless. Whoever you are, we all have something in common. We have a stressful life, and we're suffering from within, wanting to get out.

You try to fit in with your friends and family, you try to be calm and pretend that everything is fine, but even though your friends and family seem to be there, you know deep in your heart that they don't know what you're going through. They ask you questions like, "Are you okay?", only to respond with, "It'll be okay," to whatever it is you tell them. Why do they even ask? Isn't it obvious that you're not okay? Sure, it'll be okay, but definitely not today.

You may find yourself using different substances, like alcohol, cigarettes, and recreational drugs, trying to numb the pain and relieve the stress. But when you sober up, you find that your problems are still there. They haven't moved a bit; sometimes, they've even gotten worse. Some of you force yourselves not to be sober, or you try to find new ways to cope by shopping or binge eating. Nevertheless, you never find yourself truly happy. Some of you even go out of your way for happiness, doing things like going back to school, frequenting bars, chatting online, hanging out with friends, or even cheating on your spouse.

Unfortunately, no one can be told what it's like living the life that's simple and easy. There are no words that can describe it, but I can try my best to give you a close analogy. Have you ever gone to a religious weekend retreat? At this type of retreat, you may feel cleansed of sin; as if the love of the Higher Power is so close that you can almost touch it. You may feel elevated to a whole new level, but the Monday following that weekend retreat will feel very different. You may feel a sense of invincibility. You may think that you can tackle anything and everything that comes at you, and that you can forgive anyone who wrongs you. You almost feel like you're Superman. The feeling doesn't last, though. In a few days, everything will be back to normal. Routines will go back to where they were, and the stress will slowly creep back in. That feeling I just described, the sense of invincibility, the feeling of being on a different level, is the closest I can get to describing the life this book can show you. And it's still not even close to how it really is.

Do You Have the Heart?

Let's go ahead and start. The fundamental dilemma of most people trying to find the better life is that they're simply not ready.

> *When the student is ready, the teacher will come.*
> – Chinese proverb

Most people never *get* ready in their lifetime. And of the small number of people that do, only a handful actually make it to the other side.

You've had so many opportunities to learn the simple life. You've heard it so many ways, in so many different forms. Some of it may have been through other books, some may have been from your parents, your friends, a counselor, a social worker, a priest, your psychiatrist, a TV show, a movie, the radio, an article in a magazine, a poem, a quote, the internet. Both you and I know that you've tried to change. You've maybe even asked Google how to do it, and you've probably clicked on 'The 5 Simple Steps to Getting Rid of Stress' or 'The 7 Easy Ways to Live Life'. Despite that, you've ended up here. Before now, you simply weren't ready, and today, you may still not have reached that state. But it's my hope that you'll become ready before the start of the next section.

Now, what does it mean to be 'ready'? It's not enough

to just want the better life. Knowing that you want that life doesn't bring it about. Knowing is only half the battle, and doing is the other half. You've tried doing it, and you know you've tried, not once, not twice, but several times. Again, you must understand that it's not as simple as that. Your mind may think that you want a better life, but your heart needs a little bit more convincing. Everyone thinks they want a better life, but no one has the heart to take a step towards it.

Have you ever really loved to do one thing? Maybe you love to dance, sing, or play an instrument? Could it be a certain sport like soccer, basketball, or football? Could it be another outdoor activity like rock climbing or kayaking? Even sit-at-home hobbies, like model trains, fixing computers, or just playing video games could be the one thing that you love. Think of something that you know you really put your heart into.

Do you notice something different inside of you, when you do this? Right now, trying to recall this, you already feel a sense of joy in you – a joy that comes from the heart. There are no words that can explain how you feel about it, but you know it's there. It's as if the world changes. Some people call this feeling that comes from your heart 'passion', some people call it 'drive'. When you have passion or drive to do a certain thing, it becomes simple and easy. Individuals who have these traits tend to be able to do more and achieve more.

The task you now have at hand is to convince your heart to want the better life in this way. I can preach to you until my face turns blue, but if you're not ready in this way, it will all be in vain.

Breaking Point

Getting ready is a process. It may be instant for some, but for most, it's a *long* process. Most people become ready when they reach their breaking point. It's the lowest point a person can possibly have; a deeply unfortunate circumstance that no one wants to be in. It's a point where we feel alone, helpless, and hopeless.

> *I tried. I tried. I tried. I tried. I tried. I'm tired.*
> – Anonymous

Everyone has a breaking point. Even the nicest of people have their limits, a maximum amount of stress that they can stand. This level is called our threshold, and the point immediately above this ultimate threshold is our breaking point. Once our stress level surpasses our threshold, we reach this breaking point, and we declare ourselves officially broken. This is usually the point at which the soup hits the fan. At this stage, people can go one of two ways. They either give up or open up. You've heard in the news of people breaking down, especially during the economic meltdown of 2008. Sometimes, it's the people you least suspect of breaking down who are the ones that suffer worst. Now, I don't want you to give up. Rather, I want you to open up.

The goal of the general population is to avoid reaching this breaking point. You'll find many self-help books that can show you how to keep yourself from reaching that point. However, this book is not your ordinary, run-of-the-mill self-help manual. The goal of this week is to assist you in reaching this breaking point, in order to become ready.

The authors were once in situations similar to yours; not exactly the same, but believe us when we say that we, too, suffered and we, too, had to reach breaking point to become ready. Conrad, in particular, took a really long time to get there – to reach rock bottom.

"It was when every single thing in my life was just wrong, where every single thing that I did was a mistake. But even at rock bottom, I wasn't ready, because everyone knows that once you hit rock bottom, there's nowhere to go but up. So I waited around, I tried to make myself comfortable where I was. Apparently, when you hit rock bottom, there's nowhere else to go but sideways, not up. But even sick and tired of going sideways, I wasn't ready. After a while, a considerably long while, I became sick and tired of being sick and tired. *That* was my breaking point, and finally, I was ready."

Most people have to undergo a similar process to reach their breaking point. However, for a few, it only takes one sudden, significant change in their lives to throw them over the threshold. This happens when, all of a sudden, they hit their heads and wake up realizing that they need to make a change. A good example of this is a near-death experience. People who survive accidents, cancer, or other serious conditions get a sudden jolt. Out of nowhere, they know that their lives could have been cut short, and they abruptly reach their breaking point. They realize something like 'life is too short to waste', and they make that step towards change. For other people, it could be a drastic change in circumstance. It can be a loved one leaving you, or jail time, loss of job, debt, health, infidelity, family issues, or task saturation, any of which can put someone over the threshold.

Reaching this breaking point is a depressing but necessary step to achieving the life you seek. Why is it so important to reach this point before a person can become ready? Before I can answer that question, we first need to know what happens at breaking point. Two things happen – realization and acceptance. Let us tackle each separately.

Realization

What is it that we need to realize? People who have reached their breaking point realize that their lives aren't working. You may say that the reason you're reading this book is because you know your life is disappointing, but knowing that, right now, is superficial. Most of the stress that we have in ourselves is in the subconscious. The stress that we think we have now is only the tip of the iceberg.

When we look at another person's disappointing life as a stranger, or from a third-person point of view, we can quickly identify the stressors and have a more objective idea of what's really going on with them. A good example of this is substance abuse. People who abuse alcohol will deny that they have a problem, despite the fact that there are so many indications and so many people pointing them out. In the same way that they can't see their situation clearly, it's difficult for us to see our own. We've dug ourselves into such a deep hole that we don't even realize there *is* a hole.

When people break, the realization of their disappointing life is much more profound. This is the moment when everything surfaces. They realize that their life isn't just disappointing, but depressing, displeasing, frustrating, inadequate, uninteresting, and whatever other negative words you can think of. It's when every little stress comes out in the open, including the tiniest irritations. Our nerves are exposed, and everything is now part of our issues. It's somehow become a part of all that we cannot stand about our life. The gas prices, the screeching brakes in the car, the seemingly successful, happy lives of others. We say so many things and ask so many questions like,

"Why does this always happen to me?", "Why can't I hit the lottery?", "Why can't things go my way for once?", "Why does no one understand me?", "Am I going to be like this for the rest of my life?"

The process of deep realization regarding our disappointing lives may take a while. We continue to deny it until we reach the threshold. After that, we just say, "Yes, my life, in fact, sucks."

Acceptance

The second thing that occurs at breaking point is acceptance. People who break have learned to accept that anything and everything they've done, or tried to do, simply hasn't worked. They've tried every trick in the book to get a better life, they've done their very best, but it's as if they're going in circles, always winding up back at square one.

One of the reasons we're unable to accept this is because we always hang on to hope – hope of a better future, hope of a better life, or even hope of a better afterlife. This hope blinds us to what we're experiencing in the present. We continue to move on with the hope that everything will eventually be okay. Someday, not today, but someday, everything will be okay, and the hope of that better tomorrow makes today livable. Sometimes, this hope is so strong that it even makes us happy. However, this tomorrow never comes.

People live through many 'tomorrows' and yet end up where they were before. That's 365 tomorrows every year, and 3,650 tomorrows every decade. As of writing, the average American lifespan is approximately 79 years. That's 28,835 tomorrows, none of which bring the better life. And that's only life; people who believe in an afterlife hope that they'll have the life they seek once all those tomorrows run out. That means, as long as they're alive, there's no real hope for a better situation.

Let's go over a few examples of how people cope with the stresses of life – how they try to make their lives better. One way to do this is through rationalization.

We rationalize to make our lives seem reasonable. Sometimes we try to say to ourselves that our life is 'okay', because we know that there are other people who have it worse. We try to visualize individuals who are less fortunate than us, which makes life seem better. We thank the Higher Power for giving us the life that we have, because there are people in third-world countries who are literally just trying to survive.

However, this type of thinking also promotes the idea that there are people who have it better than us. We don't need to manifest these individuals in our minds, because we see them every day – at work, in our neighborhood, on our commute – and knowing that there are people better than us makes our lives seem inferior.

Another, similar concept is being contented. "Be

content with what you have," they say. This statement has the same premise; we make it seem that we don't want anything more than what we currently have. But we all want something more, don't we? It's difficult to suppress our wants when we see advertisements for every new thing out there – new clothes, shoes, phones, etc., even before we start trying to keep up with the Joneses.

Both these concepts make us suppress the reality of what we actually want. It could be a better phone, new clothes, a new car, a better job, or something else, but you and I both know it's not that easy. Somewhere deep within us, it wants to come out.

Thinking positive is yet another way to rationalize our lives. We try our best to find something positive in our situation – the silver lining. Some, if not most, of the time, it's not possible, especially when we find ourselves in horrible circumstances. It's not simple, nor is it easy.

Even though we can find a silver lining, thinking positive only emphasizes that there really are negatives. It's like having a sweet lemon – it doesn't change the fact that life is a lemon, and you want it to be something else. When you think positive, you suppress the negative feelings into your subconscious. Doing that is very unhealthy; I know you've heard of that very positive person who eventually broke down because they were hiding all those negative emotions and reached their threshold. Another idea for trying to keep those negative feelings at bay is, "Don't sweat the small stuff." We know these little things can easily pile up and become a monster inside us. Thinking positive is very negative.

These concepts of rationalization are ways in which we deliberately lie to ourselves to make our lives seem bearable, suppressing all our wants, needs, and negative feelings. I think it's pretty obvious that this simply doesn't work.

Another way in which we make our lives bearable is through distraction. We think that if we can distract ourselves from our stressful lives, even for a moment, it will make our situation livable. Distractions come in several different forms. Some people do yoga or meditation, some focus on sports or hobbies, some use alcohol or a smoke break, some look forward to the long weekend or a vacation, and some just take that extra time in the potty. But the most common way Americans distract themselves is by watching television. Keeping up with the latest shows, movies, or current events entertains us enough to keep our minds from our stressful lives. When we get back to it, we feel somewhat refreshed, ready to take another beating. Unfortunately, distractions only relieve us of the stress for a brief period of time. After the entertainment is over, we sigh in disappointment, knowing that we have to go back to our depressing lives.

One way to actually deal with our overly stressful lives is by taking it one day at a time. Don't dwell on the past and don't worry about the future – two things that rob us of today. By focusing only on today, we try to break larger problems into smaller pieces that make them easier to tackle. However, we become narrow-sighted, like race horses with blinders; we address our stresses for one day, but we don't solve the problem of life. What happens here is that only temporary solutions or fixes are created, instead of looking at the bigger picture and getting to the real root of the problem. Another dead end.

Some even say that stress is an important part of our lives. A little bit of stress every day can keep us on our toes and keep us going, right? If that's the case, then there's absolutely no way in which we can eliminate stress. Our lives will always be stressful.

Another reason we struggle is that we're unable to accept failure. Are we just supposed to give up? Are we supposed to admit that nothing works? But the better question to ask is, "Why not?" A lot of people are too ignorant to know when they're beaten. When things are going wrong, we continue to do the same things to fix a situation, thinking it will change. There has to be a point where we say, "Hey, this isn't working." We need to scrap the idea or the whole thing altogether and accept that it's just not going to work, no matter what we do. It's like a toddler trying to fit a square object in a round hole – it just doesn't work.

A person who has broken down has accepted that

nothing works. Everything we try to do seems ineffective. It doesn't relieve any of our stresses, especially the ones deep within ourselves.

The Fractus

Let's admit it: it seems like life was designed for failure. It's practically undeniable that people will eventually reach their breaking point. It's not a matter of if, it's only a matter of when. Most of us, though, will die before we reach that point, and it's only in that breaking point that a breakthrough becomes possible. That means most of us will never get to see the world how it should be seen and live life how it should be lived.

Going back to what we said earlier; it's not enough for you to think you want the better life. Your heart must be strong enough to go through the process. At breaking point, it's not only the mind that breaks; your heart breaks with it. We don't realize it, but the power of our hearts is greater than that of our minds. When you have the passion or drive to do something, your heart has the ability to achieve anything and break boundaries.

> *You can lead a horse to water, but you can't make it drink.*
> – Anonymous

Once you've come to a deep realization of your extremely stressful life, and accepted the fact that nothing that you've done works, the heart starts to open up. When all of these things happen together, like an orchestra playing a symphony, this is the time you're truly ready. There are no words to describe this situation. So, we will refer to this orchestration with the term 'fractus'. It's the goal of this section to help you achieve fractus.

Life Should Be Simple and Easy

I know that there are several ways to live life. Since every single one of us is a unique individual, we can live life in as many ways as there are people in the world.

There are a hundred ways to skin a cat.
– Anonymous

I, however, have found the one way that is simplest and easiest, which means that the '99' other ways are more difficult than the one. This is the reason I want you to open up. 99% of people do the same old routine, following the same old ways and the same old methods of eliminating the stresses of life. If you keep on doing what 99% of people do, you'll never find the happiness you so desperately want to achieve.

But what is it that 1% of people do to attain this life

of simplicity and ease? This is what I'll discuss in the weeks to come. As the book unfolds, you'll find that it's not a secret, it's just the truth. They say that the truth hurts, and it will, but it's still the truth. These truths will challenge most, if not all, of your beliefs – beliefs about money, religion, and life. They also say that the truth will set you free – that's certainly true here, but it will hurt like hell to get there. Nevertheless, if you finally come to agree with these truths, you'll achieve a life that is simple, a life that is easy.

Summary

This first week, I understand, is a depressing one. However, I cannot emphasize enough that it's a necessary part of the process. You have to realize and accept that life is, in fact, broken, and reach the state of fractus. I assure you that, when you finally attain this life, you'll be able to live free of rationalizations. It's a life where you won't need to think positive to be positive. It's a life where you will be free of negative feelings. It's a life where you won't need to be content to be happy. It's a life where you learn from the past so you can change the future. It's a life that you can take as a whole, not in small, day-by-day pieces. It's a life where you don't want to be distracted. It's a life that you want to have complete focus on, every single waking moment. It's a life where you don't need to cope because, ultimately, it's a life that's free of stress.

As you continue to read, everything in this book should make logical sense. If it doesn't make sense, it shouldn't be in the book. However, as explained earlier, what you'll read will also prove to be outside of the 99% – outside of the norm. It will sound abnormal, crazy even, but it will still make logical sense, and it will still be the truth. That's why you must have an open mind when reading this book; because only when you're ready will you be able to have this life. After all, if you're doing it hard, you're doing it wrong.

Let me end this section with a quote commonly attributed to Albert Einstein.

> *Insanity is doing the same thing over and over and expecting different results.*
> – Albert Einstein

Exercises

As mentioned in the preface, this book isn't meant to be read from front to back in one sitting. Now, I pass the ball to you. This is where your journey begins.

In the coming week, your goal is to reach the state of fractus. It may not be a literal breaking point that others have gone through, but hopefully a similar situation wherein you will experience the same realization and acceptance that will result in action.

In this process, you'll need to open up. You don't have to open up to me, but you will have to open up to yourself. You'll be in a safe place within your own mind, a place where you can be down-and-dirty honest with yourself. I won't judge you, and nor will other people. I have to warn you, though, that there will be one person who'll judge you. It will be yourself.

You may not be aware of it, but it will be difficult to accept certain facts. This is your life; you have poured sweat and blood for so many years to get to where you are now, and it may seem like I've come here to tear everything down. If you feel like you're not quite ready to go down that road, this is a good point at which to put down the book. Put it in a place nearby, so that someday, when you feel ready, you can pick it back up and start your journey. Otherwise, let's continue.

The stress that you feel right now is just the tip of the iceberg. You'll need to pull out the whole iceberg to reach fractus. Examine yourself. Dig deep into yourself. What are the stressors in your life? Think of every single stress that you feel – from the tiniest to the largest – and let them all out. Look for your deepest stresses, fears, and anxieties. Is it your significant other, your coworker, your mother? Think of how they contribute to your stress. Is it the way your spouse nags at you every day? Is it the way your co-worker acts? Is it your financial situation? Think about your past. Is your past still haunting you, even in the smallest of ways? Are you worried about the future? Are you anxious that something may not turn out in your favor? Live your life for at least a week. Try to identify each and every stressor that you encounter. Make a diary if you'd like.

After you've listed your stressors, look into how you've tried to avoid or cope with the resultant stress. Did you try to rationalize to yourself? Did you try to distract yourself? Did you try to use blinders? Or maybe you've tried something else. Where are you now? With the different ways you've used to try and cope with the stress, do you feel like you've progressed? Or does it feel like you're running in circles? More importantly, do you still feel the stress of life? Are those negative feelings building up inside, waiting to burst out? Is it still difficult to get out of bed on Monday, or every day, for that matter? Does is feel like you're doing the same old routine, just on a different day? Are you about ready to accept and admit that nothing works? Give it another week if you'd like. Go ahead and try different ways of dealing with stress and try to find what works.

Give it as much time as you need to consider yourself officially broken. It's okay to feel alone, helpless, and hopeless, but it's not okay to lie to yourself. You don't have to convince me that you're ready; you have to convince your heart that it's ready and willing. Only then can you open yourself up to other possibilities – possibilities outside of the norm. Through realization and acceptance, your heart can open up, and only then can you reach the state of fractus. Only then can you be ready. One last question you need to ask yourself: "Am I ready to let go of everything I know?"

Pause

NOTES

_____

_____

_____

_____

_____

_____

_____

_____

_____

_____

_____

_____

_____

_____

_____

_____

_____

_____

_____

_____

_____

_____

_____

_____

Life Should Be Simple and Easy

Week 2

The Past Determines Today

Recap

It's been one whole week since the last section, and I applaud you for coming this far. Not everyone reaches this point – the state of fractus. As I stated in the previous week, it's important to realize that life is broken and accept that our previous actions didn't bear fruit. This means we can move forward and learn what 99% do not.

I want to remind you that, from this point onward, I will only state the truth. There will be truths that may be difficult to accept, but they will be truths nonetheless. Being in the state of fractus will aid you in opening your mind and especially your heart to these truths. So, I will try my best to explain these truths in a way that makes sense.

This Week's Content

In order to learn something complex, we need to start with the basics. Just like with any sport, one must train from the beginning. In American football, for example, the players have to learn the rules and regulations of the game, then they choose a position in the field they want to play. Later, they do muscle training, running, throwing, catching, arm exercises, leg exercises, etc. This helps improve their strength, speed, and coordination. They train for these aspects separately, but they unite as a whole when they play the game, which helps them win.

As we start on your journey to the life that's simple and easy, it's therefore necessary to start with the basics. In doing so, I aim to identify the source of your stress – the origin. Once we identify it, we can then work towards how we can make it disappear. First, I'll introduce several basic concepts, then I'll build up towards more complex ones. Some of these concepts may not seem immediately applicable to your present situation, but if you stay the course, they will aid you as it all comes together.

Knowledge and Intelligence

In this section, I'll discuss how people are created. I don't mean in the biological sense, but how you, as a person, become who you are – the essence of what makes us human. What sets us apart from animals is our ability to process thought – human intelligence.

intelligence
the ability to acquire and apply knowledge and skills
– Oxford Dictionary

Although knowledge is a term commonly used alongside intelligence, it has its own distinct meaning.

knowledge
facts, information, and skills acquired by a person through experience or education; the theoretical or practical understanding of a subject
– Oxford Dictionary

Knowledge is merely information stored in the brain, but intelligence is how we use that information. It isn't our ability to store information that makes us human, but the way we process it. This is just like a car; even if I have all the pieces of a car in a large bucket, they still won't function as a car.

> *Knowledge isn't power until it is applied.*
> – Dale Carnegie, *How to Stop Worrying and Start Living*

Human Behavior

Once we process information in our brain and put it into action, it becomes human behavior. Behavior includes every action you perform – the way you move, the way you speak, the way you think, and even the way you process information. This is what makes you who you are. However, there's a misconception about what behavior actually is. Most people think that behavior is innate, that it comes from within. That's why you hear the expression, "Be true to yourself and just be who you are." But the real question is, "Who are we, really?"

If you don't know who you are, people will say, "Find yourself, from within." How, exactly, are you supposed to do that? How does one dig deep within oneself to find out who one really is? This book will not tell you to do such a thing. It's simply impossible. In fact, it's a myth.

99% think: Human behavior is innate or inborn.

This is why 'finding yourself' cannot give you inner peace. My goal is to show you how people are created – how human behavior is created, and what makes you who you are. Human behavior, however, is a very complex subject, and I won't be diving too deep into the details. Still, by the end of this section, you will hopefully understand the basics. An understanding of human behavior lies in one simple principle.

1% think: Human behavior is learned.

Every single one of us has a unique set of DNA; genes that code who we are. Some people were born to be more this, or more that, or less this, less that. Each one of us may look anatomically different based on our DNA. We'll have different skin color, eye color, height, gender, even anatomically different internal organs. Some may have a larger stomach, while others may have a unique vein distribution or a more efficient liver. There are three billion base pairs in the human genome, and an almost infinite number of combinations that make us unique. We may even have a unique morphology of the brain: larger or smaller, more or fewer grooves. Despite this, we all have one thing in common. We were all created with a blank slate or a 'tabula rasa'.

tabula rasa

a mind not yet affected by experiences, impressions, etc.

anything existing undisturbed in its original, pure state

– Merriam-Webster Dictionary

Every one of us starts with a blank mind, but as we grow, we acquire information and store it in our minds. We then learn to use these pieces of information. When we're babies, we learn how to get food, but it *is* a learning process.

Now, picture yourself as a baby. The first piece of information that baby will have is the sensation of hunger or thirst. The very first time that baby feels this sensation, they don't know what it is, or what to do about it. All they can perceive is discomfort. The baby doesn't even know that the sensation is actually 'hunger' or 'thirst'.

What happens next is the way the baby tries to process this information. The infant can choose to do several different things. It can wait for the sensation to disappear on its own or it can try to move or reposition itself, but it will eventually try to communicate, and the only way the baby can communicate is to cry. The parents don't see the other options the baby may have chosen to alleviate the discomfort, because crying is the only perceivable response.

The process by which the baby chooses its options

may happen within seconds; as the baby runs through its options, it will eventually see which option doesn't work and which one does – which causes its mother to help it.

After this happens for the very first time, the baby doesn't instantly know to cry for milk, nor will it know that it is 'hungry'. Right now, the baby is just content that a certain sensation of discomfort has been alleviated. This process will then occur several more times. Through repetition, the baby will eventually instantaneously cry at this sensation. Even then, the baby doesn't know it is 'hungry'. The baby will also undergo this process with other types of discomfort, like a wet diaper, pain, or sleepiness.

As the baby grows, it will undergo this same process as it learns to walk, talk, run, and potty. Then, as a child, it will learn to play and study. As a teen, to dress and make friends. As an adult, to drive, work, cook, budget, invest, and love. It has been documented that learning can start even before birth, in the mother's womb.

Give me a dozen healthy infants, well-formed, and my own specified world to bring them up in and I'll guarantee to take any one at random and train him to become any type of specialist I might select – doctor, lawyer, artist, merchant-chief and, yes, even beggar-man and thief, regardless of his talents, penchants, tendencies, abilities, vocations, and race of his ancestors. I am going

beyond my facts, and I admit it, but so have the advocates of the contrary, and they have been doing it for many thousands of years.
– Watson, *Behaviorism*, 1925

John B. Watson received his Ph.D. in psychology from the University of Chicago in 1903. After years of research and study, he published his book, *Behaviorism*, in 1925. His writing makes perfect sense. Every person can be molded into whatever you want them to be. We become who we are through constant learning; a process we call 'life'.

There were two other psychologists who made such major contributions to the study of human behavior – Ivan Pavlov and B.F. Skinner. Ivan Pavlov won the Nobel Prize in Physiology in 1904. He was a Russian physiologist who did research on classical conditioning, perhaps gaining his dogs more fame than he achieved for himself. The most famous experiment was feeding his dogs while associating a particular sound, like a bell or a buzzer, with the act. Every time Pavlov presented food, he rang the bell. After repeating this multiple times, Pavlov rang the bell without giving food to the dogs. The dogs still salivated, conditioned to associate the sound of the bell with food. This type of learning is called classical conditioning.

We wake up at a designated time from Monday to Friday. On the weekend, even if we don't set our alarms, we wake up at around the same time. This is a conditioned response. Many of us have also conditioned ourselves such that we cannot start our day without coffee. There are many things we do which stem from classical conditioning, and Pavlov's study of classical conditioning has rightly enjoyed significant influence in the field of psychology and behaviorism.

Another major process of learning is through operant conditioning. B.F. Skinner was an American psychologist awarded the National Medal of Science in behavioral and social science in 1968. Skinner proposed the idea that people learn by means of reinforcement. He built a cage called the operant chamber. This chamber had several levers and switches which could trigger a number of different responses, varying from delivery of food, an electric shock, light, sound, or a combination of these. The basic idea was that these switches would either produce a positive or a negative response. Skinner would then place an animal in the chamber, and it would eventually trigger the levers and switches. The animal would not immediately learn a switch's purpose on its first activation, but through continued repetition, they would learn to use the lever with the positive response and to avoid the switch with the negative response.

Just like housebreaking an animal, positive or negative feedback is used to shape behavior. It's the same way we potty-train our children. Many things we do, we learned through operant conditioning.

Image by Curtis Neveu, distributed under a CC BY-SA 3.0 license, via Wikimedia Commons

Every aspect of behavior is learned. And most, if not all, of these aspects are learned through these two types of conditioning, or a combination thereof.

We cannot teach a child what the word 'hot' means. No matter how elaborately you put it into words, we are incapable of *showing* what it means. The child will have to touch a hot surface to know what 'hot' is, and this will constitute negative reinforcement through heat, even pain.

The child may not learn to avoid a hot surface immediately and may need repetition to finally learn not to touch that particular hot surface. Now that the child knows not to touch that hot surface, how will the child know not to touch other hot surfaces? Well, we associate the situation with a word – 'hot'. Every time the child touches any hot surface, we mention the word 'hot'. At this point, the child will learn to associate the word 'hot' with the sensation of heat. Now, every time you say the word 'hot', the child knows not to touch what you identify as 'hot', even if that is not a hot surface.

Gifts and Talents

I could continue giving examples, but the idea I want you to understand is that every single behavior is learned. Let's go back to the idea of John B. Watson; that he can make anything out of a child – a doctor, an artist, or a thief. This theory has been proven several times before. One good example is talent. We usually think of talent as inborn or innate, but it isn't. Talent is learned. It's often driven by interest. If the person has a genuine interest in a certain sport, that person will want to learn it, and with the right time and effort, that person will be able to achieve an Olympic gold medal. If we only needed raw talent to win the gold, it would be so easy to be an Olympic athlete, but that's not the case. It takes years of practice. Then again, practice doesn't make perfect; *correct* practice makes perfect.

Do you know what 'kung fu' means? Contrary to popular belief, it doesn't mean 'martial arts'. The word 'kung' means work or effort, and 'fu' means time. The real Chinese meaning of 'kung fu' is any skill or art that is mastered through time and effort. Kung fu masters are only masters of time and effort, and anything can be learned with the proper time and effort.

Previously, the Russian Federation was the Union of Soviet Socialist Republics or USSR, also known as the Soviet Union. We know the Soviet Union for their strict communist government. As the USSR, they joined the Olympic Games from 1952 to 1988. Since the Olympic Games are held every four years, with the exception of the 1984 boycott, the Soviets entered eight games. Of the eight times, they ranked first in six of them. The reason wasn't pure talent or being 'gifted'. No; their athletes were strictly trained. In a communist country, these athletes were forced into becoming the athletes that they were. It simply proves that any person, with the right training, can achieve the same results.

Even the way we walk is learned. The way we dress, the way we brush our teeth, the way we view other people and other cultures, the things we find funny, the things we think are cool. Even our language is learned. Not just which language we speak, like English, Spanish, or French, but the manner in which we choose our words. It's easy for us to associate behavior with only the actions we can see, but as I stated earlier, human behavior includes all of our actions. These actions include the way we think and the way we process thoughts. These actions are unseen by the human eye, but they are actions nonetheless, and these actions are also learned.

Emotions

Now, I want to go a little bit further into the unseen actions, into emotions. Emotions are also actions. Emotions are human reactions to certain events or situations.

> **emotion**
> *the affective aspect of consciousness*
> *a state of feeling*
> *a conscious mental reaction (as anger or fear) subjectively experienced as strong feeling usually directed toward a specific object and typically accompanied by physiological and behavioral changes in the body*
> – Merriam-Webster Dictionary

Believe it or not, our emotions don't come from the heart. The manner in which we experience emotion makes it seem like it's a natural reaction. Our whole body feels the emotion.

99% think: Emotions are natural human reactions.

When we are angry, our eyes open wider, our blood boils, we feel the heat flowing through our veins, our arm has the urge to hit something, our voice gets louder, our heart pumps stronger and faster, our breathing becomes deeper. The same thing happens with other emotions. It's a whole-body experience, whether you are joyful, sad, or embarrassed. Despite this, emotion is indeed a complex brain function.

1% think: Emotions are part of our thought process.

The way we express our emotions is learned as early as late infancy. As a child, we start to learn that a smile from our parents is a sign of acceptance. It's a positive experience which shows that the child's actions are accepted. On the other hand, if the child does something wrong, the parent may shout at the child, where the loud volume becomes a negative experience and is a sign of rejection.

As an adult, through years of learning, we express our emotions differently. Crying as an infant can mean several different things. It can mean that the baby is hungry, wet, in pain, or sleepy. As the child grows, develops, and learns, crying will evolve to become the means to express sorrow or pain.

You have that someone in your life who says they're happy but doesn't look happy at all. Then there's that someone who looks like they're happy, despite negative events in their life, or another who doesn't know how to get mad. These are extremes in the spectrum, and I bring them up to exhibit the fact that emotions are learned. It's not *just* the emotion that is learned, however; the event or situation that triggers the emotion is learned, too.

What triggers you to be happy or sad is unique to what others may perceive to be joyful or sorrowful. One extreme example is the masochist. The masochist finds pleasure in their own pain or humiliation. You may say that this is one sick person, but this is simply what they learned. As a child, perhaps, he or she was abused. Then, the abuser rewarded the child. This provided the child with a form of positive feedback, teaching that pain and humiliation are good things. Through repetition, masochism takes root just like any other 'natural' tendency.

Summary

Everything is learned, and I mean *every* aspect of human behavior. What we love and what we hate is learned. So, when I say that the past will determine today, I mean that every action, reaction, and non-action is based on what you have learned (and not learned) in the past, including all your experiences, through repetitive classic conditioning, through reinforcement, or through other methods. Now, if everything we think, say, or do is learned, then when we're presented with a situation, we can only act in a certain way, directed by what we have learned.

99% think: When a person is taught, that person will learn.

Learning is a process. Merely teaching a person doesn't mean that the person will learn; not everyone in calculus class will learn calculus. There will be varying degrees of learning. You may teach your children the same way, but they won't learn the same way, and one child may not even learn at all.

1% think: Teaching does not automatically result in learning. 'Knowing' it doesn't mean that a person has 'learned' it.

Exercises

Let's take a pause, right here. I don't want you to believe what this week presents as fact. Just because I mentioned a Nobel Prize winner doesn't make it true. Instead, I want you to investigate for yourself. Experiment with it. I want you to find out on your own whether what I say is true. Be the scientist or investigator you always wanted to be.

First off, look at yourself. Look at your actions. Inspect the way you act and the way you react. List the things you love and hate. Analyze the way you think and the way you choose your words. Feel your emotions. Scrutinize every action and reaction, from the biggest to the smallest, both positive and negative, from the moment you wake up to the moment you fall asleep. Dig into the roots of these thoughts and actions. How did you learn them? Make a list and run through it. Try to identify the source of these behaviors.

Think about how you were brought up by your parents. Think of your friends and peers, and how they influenced you as you grew up. Think of how television or the internet affect the way you think. You'll find that there's nothing you do now that you haven't learned to do.

How did you learn negative behaviors? Knowing which behavior is negative, why didn't you correct it? You were taught to engage in positive behaviors through your family and religion, but why weren't the lessons total; how did negative behaviors flourish?

Now, examine other people. Why do you think your coworker said this, or your friend thinks of you that way? Observe the way they move, the way they react. How do you think they learned this? Interrogate them if you wish. Ask them how they were brought up. What was their background?

After you figure out that all of us operate on previously learned concepts, the better question to ask is if you were taught to act a certain way, who taught the people who taught you? And who taught them? And so on, and so forth.

Pause

NOTES

_____
_____
_____
_____
_____
_____
_____
_____
_____
_____
_____
_____
_____
_____
_____
_____
_____
_____
_____
_____
_____
_____
_____
_____
_____
_____

Week 3

What is Real?

Recap

Now, **at least two weeks** have gone by. Congratulate yourself on being able to persevere and continue the book. In the first week, I made you ready – ready to open your mind to possibilities outside of the 99% by entering the state of fractus.

Last week, we started to discuss the origin of our thoughts. You, now, understand that everything you think of and do not think of is only a result of what you have learned, or not learned, throughout the years of your life. This will help you appreciate that the concepts which follow are also learned, the same way that you have learned everything else.

This Week's Content

This section contains the central concept of the whole book. The truths revealed in this section are vital, and together they form the path to identifying the origin of your stress. For this reason, it's essential that you understand them; if $a=b$, and $b=c$, then $a=c$. To make this journey, however, we have to understand what each of those letters mean. Although it may sound philosophical, I only aim to show you the truth, nothing else.

What is Real?

> ***real***
> *actually existing or happening*
> *not imaginary*
> – Merriam-Webster Dictionary

What makes something real? How do we know that something is real? How can we confirm that it's real? It's easy to believe that something is real if we can use our senses to prove it, but there are things in this world that we cannot confirm in that way.

> *What is real? How do you define real? If you're talking about what you can feel, what you can smell, what you can taste and see, then real is simply electrical signals interpreted by your brain.*
> – Morpheus, *The Matrix*, 1999

When we dream, we stimulate the same parts of the brain. Everything in our dream feels so real. You think you can use your senses in your dream; you see and you touch in the same way, yet this doesn't help you identify the dream for what it is. You move in your dream as if it was real, but you wake up the next morning knowing that it was only a dream. It *wasn't* real – just electrical signals in your brain.

We don't realize it, but our brain is a powerful organ. As we continue in this section, I hope you'll gain a better understanding of what's real and what isn't.

Seeing the Light

Did you know that visible light only accounts for a tiny fraction of the spectrum of electromagnetic waves we use

If You're Doing It Hard, You're Doing It Wrong

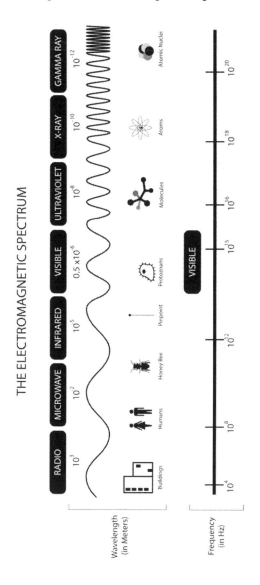

THE ELECTROMAGNETIC SPECTRUM

Image by Jonathan S. Urie distributed under a CC BY-SA 3.0 license, via Wikimedia Commons

every day? Despite the fact that we don't see other types of electromagnetic waves, we still believe they're real because we *can* see their consequences. X-rays can show bone structure, microwaves are used to heat up food, and other types of useful electromagnetic wave allow for Bluetooth, GPS, NFC, Wi-Fi, television broadcast, radar detection, ultraviolet markings, infrared heat identification, and more.

The actual electromagnetic waves are invisible to the human eye. Moreover, these waves don't bear mass or weight. Therefore, we cannot use our five senses to confirm that they're real. Let's take a small pause to digest that thought for a moment.

> *Except for visible light, electromagnetic waves are invisible to the human eye and don't bear mass or weight.*

Do you understand the gravity of that idea? There are things which exist that you cannot see, hear, touch, taste, or smell. It defies all of what we know about 'real'. But they still exist, and they're still real.

There are more real things that are difficult to identify than just electromagnetic waves. My philosophy teacher once explained how, when we draw a circle on a piece of paper, it won't be a perfect circle. Even if we use a compass to draw it, it will never be perfect, yet a perfect circle exists in your mind. We know that a circle is a set of points on a plane that are all at a given distance, the radius, from a given point, the center. This idea is the concept of a circle. You cannot draw a perfect circle, but your mind has an idea of the perfect circle. It's a concept that is very real, and a concept that can only exist in our minds.

At this very moment, you have a picture in your mind of the perfect circle. This image of the circle in your mind is not visible to the human eye, it doesn't bear mass or weight, but it *is* real. It's as real as electromagnetic waves. Now, if this concept of the perfect circle can exist, what prevents other concepts from existing?

Abstract Thought

Abstract words, like 'justice' and 'love', are concepts that we know exist, even if they're difficult to explain. Have you ever been asked the question, "How do you define love?"

It's difficult to define love because it's not something tangible or visible. It doesn't bear mass or weight, but you know it's there. There are different kinds of love: love of family, love of a partner, love of a friend, love of a pet, etc. No matter what kind of love, it's still the same word. Now, think of someone or something you love. Just by bringing that love to mind, you feel something. Even though we can't see it, touch it, smell it, or taste it, we know it's real. Like the electromagnetic waves, we can only see the result.

We are able to comprehend abstract words like 'liberty', 'opportunity', 'forgiveness', 'opinion', and 'faith'. The words may not be real, but the concepts behind them *are*. Just because we cannot draw the perfect circle doesn't mean it isn't real.

Beliefs and the Truth

Single, abstract words, on their own, are difficult enough to define, but once we put multiple abstract words together, we create an even more complicated concept. These concepts become part of our beliefs, forming the basis of culture, religion, and society.

> **belief**
> *a feeling of being sure that someone or something exists or that something is true*
> – Merriam-Webster Dictionary

We live in the world with the idea that these concepts are real. We act and react, thinking that our beliefs are true. But are they?

> *There are three sides to every story – yours, mine, and the truth.*
> – Robert Evans

How can we confirm that our beliefs are actually true? You have your own beliefs and other people have theirs, and then there's the truth. What makes you think that *your* beliefs are real and true?

99% think: Their beliefs are the only true beliefs.

You may have believed in Santa Claus when you were a kid. I'd like you to think back to those times – times when Santa was real. You believed in Santa and had faith that he would bring you presents at Christmas if you were on the 'nice' list. No one could prove that Santa Claus existed, but you believed nonetheless. How could he not be real? You received presents every single Christmas from Santa! You may have tried to stay up late until Santa arrived, or at least listened for the sleigh bells as he flew by, and you probably even left him milk and cookies that he ate and drank. How could he *not* be real? We believed Santa was real because this was what we learned to believe. Until we figured it out, we continued to believe such – our belief made it real. It was as real as the abstract words, as real as the perfect circle, as real as electromagnetic waves. It didn't bear mass or weight, but it was real.

As a kid, it was easy to see how Santa wasn't real when you saw your father sneaking the gift under the tree, or when your mother finally said that Santa couldn't afford presents that year, or you heard it from your elder sibling or a classmate.

1% think: Beliefs are only learned, therefore unlikely to be real or true.

Just like the little kid who believes in Santa, we believe in myriad concepts and beliefs. Sadly, there's no longer anyone we can discover sneaking gifts under the tree, no one to say that they can't afford to continue the belief, no one to tell you that it's not real. We believe in these concepts because we learned to believe in them, the same way we learned to believe in Santa. How can I contradict these beliefs? These beliefs are as real as presents every year from Santa – we can see, for ourselves, that someone has consumed the milk and cookies. So, how can our beliefs not be real? We don't question these beliefs, we don't question the origin of these beliefs, we just believe they're real. We believe they're true.

I'm not here to contradict your beliefs; I'm merely showing you how beliefs are created. Our parents started to show us the way, then everyone else around us confirmed their teachings. But who showed our parents, and who showed their parents? What is the origin of these beliefs?

In Week 2, we discussed how human behavior is learned, including the way we think and the beliefs we have. The reason there are so many different religions, cultures, societies, and forms of government is that we all grew up differently, we all learned differently. So, which one is the true belief?

Do you remember the game 'telephone', also known as 'pass the message' or 'secret message relay'? This game is where a message is passed on from one person to the next, until it gets to the end of the line. At this point, the team that has the most accurate message wins. It will never be a *perfect* message, of course. The actual message will be broken down from one person to another, the slightest error replicated and made worse with each new speaker.

This game shows how we learned our beliefs and the truths of the world we live in. These concepts and ideas have been passed on from generation to generation. Over years, decades, centuries, and even millennia, the message has been broken down, added to, taken from and modified in a variety of ways. Now, everyone has a different interpretation of this garbled message. Despite the fact that two or more people have the same religion, they may still interpret that religion differently. Because of this, it's improbable that any one of us has the true meaning of any belief.

Even the creation of a belief is difficult to keep straight. We build beliefs from words, but trying to describe an abstract word is as difficult as describing how a chocolate hazelnut cheesecake tastes. Even if I use multiple adjectives to describe it, you won't be able to understand exactly how it tastes until you put it in your mouth. How can someone have the correct idea of a word if we cannot describe a cheesecake? Despite this, we make concepts from these inadequate words, then beliefs. But these beliefs are as real as electromagnetic waves. They are as real as the perfect circle. They are as real as Santa.

Real or Verum?

You may say that this is a bunch of nonsense. Let me remind you that what you've read here isn't what the 99% think, and therefore it's not part of the norm. It will sound 'crazy', but 'crazy' doesn't mean untrue. If you have experienced the state of fractus, you're likely to have an open mind, so you're likely asking, "What is the real world?" or "How do you know what's real?"

So as not to complicate things, we'll adopt some more specific terminology. For the things and concepts that we *think* are real, we will continue to use the English term 'real'. For the things that are concrete, true, or actual, we'll use the Latin term 'verum'. Material things are verum. Things that you can detect with your senses are verum. It's the concepts that you've learned where you must question if they're real. Concepts that are real in your mind may not be verum, but that doesn't mean they're not necessary for our survival.

Governments, for example, are necessary for national and international stability and structure. We pay our taxes to the government, and the government uses these funds to build systems for us, like highways, law enforcement, etc.

But there are different types of government. You have democracies, monarchies, dictatorships, aristocracies, and others.

Religion is another belief. There are several religions out there, each one claiming to be the true religion, and each one claiming to have the real god. But religion is a necessary belief for people to connect to a Higher Power, something we'll discuss further next week.

Societies and cultures are different around the world. Our concepts of money and wealth are also beliefs. Real, perhaps, but not verum.

Reality

After a vacation, we say that we've got to go back to reality. We go back to our miserable, stressful lives. This awful life is the reality we live in, the reality we bear. We have no choice but to do it, because we have to survive, but more importantly, we have to pay the bills.

99% think: We live in the real world – a world of governments, religions, societies, and money.

Abstract words form complex concepts, multiple concepts form beliefs, and multiple beliefs form worlds. We think that the world we live in is real, but it isn't. We act like it's real, we move like it's real, we talk like it's real, but it's only real in our minds. Our mind is a powerful thing; it can create concepts that eventually form worlds. The idea of the world we live in forms our reality, which is, in turn, as real as Santa and the concept of the circle. We act in this world according to our realities, and not what is actually verum. As impossible as it may seem, our minds have created a whole world that we believe to be true. This reality blinds us to the verum.

> *1% think: The world that we live in is only the reality that we believe.*

When we dream, we create a whole world in our minds. It will take multiple computer programmers months, or even years, to build a virtual world in a video game, but we can create it overnight. That is how powerful your mind is.

The world that we live in is only an idea that we've learned to create. We've learned to live in our society, in our world, through these ideas. We learned it as we grew up – from our parents, siblings, friends, teachers, mentors, television, internet... Only one person can create these ideas in your mind – you. Even though these ideas originated in other sources, we make them real. Our minds make them real.

But why would they *not* be real, when 99% of people live in the same reality? Everyone else is confirming the reality we live in. In fact, we assume that we're all living in the same reality, but every single person lives in a unique world of their own. Every person will have different ways of growing up, different parents, siblings, friends, teachers, etc., and every person will have their own interpretation of these ideas. Your reality is yours alone, and their reality is theirs. There will be similarities, but they are not the same.

The Stress Box

99% think: Stress comes from other people or circumstances in the real world.

The reality you think of as real is the box that you create for yourself. This box is the root of all stress, because we try to fit everything into this box. Have you ever seen a toddler try to fit the star piece into a square hole? Does it work? The verum is the star piece, the box is the square hole, and we're the toddlers trying to make them fit. It won't work – the verum will not fit into our reality. What does the toddler do? The toddler will try a bit harder, then the toddler will get mad, then the toddler will cry. This sounds like a familiar tune, doesn't it? We do the exact same thing. This predicament is the source of your stress.

1% think: Stress only comes from yourself – from the creation of the stress box.

When confronted by something that doesn't fit into our reality, we wonder why it doesn't fit. Why doesn't this person understand you? Why can't they see your point of view, or see the obvious logic of your reasoning? Because you don't share the same realities! We're trying to make these people fit our reality. Most of our disagreements with other people come from not seeing eye to eye, but how is that even possible when no two people's realities are the same?

You need more money, and you're long overdue for a raise, but your boss doesn't agree. You get stressed. Why do you need more money? So, you can buy a new phone, new clothes, a new purse, a new car? Is it because you're in debt and need to pay it off? Is it because you're not rich?

Let's say you get that raise. You thank your boss, but give it a year or two and you'll soon see that it's still not enough. Why is it never enough? You perceive that you should have a life where you can purchase what you want and not worry about bills, but who said that life should be that way? Who said that you should be rich, and how rich is rich? How poor is poor? Our perception of money and wealth is real in our minds, but it isn't verum. Again, money is necessary as a means to trade goods, but the perception of wealth is the issue. How much money should you make? Is someone who makes $5 a day in a third-world country poor? And if that person is poor, is it wrong to be poor? It's not wrong to make $5 a day, but we have a negative perception of it. Your negative perception of your lack of wealth brings you stress. Who said that every American should have a television at home? Who said that you should have a car?

Your stress about your past and your future is just you trying to fit your actions (or the consequences of your actions) into your personal reality. You're trying to fit the star piece into the square hole, and it will never work. You wonder why it doesn't work, and then you get stressed. You try a bit harder, and then you get more stressed, and then you get mad, and then you get even more stressed. Eventually, you cry inside, just like that toddler. This is the cycle of stress, which eventually becomes your cycle of life.

Freedom of Choice

> *Congress shall make no law respecting an establishment of religion, or prohibiting the free exercise thereof; or abridging the freedom of speech, or of the press; or the right of the people peaceably to assemble, and to petition the government for a redress of grievances.*
> – The First Amendment, U.S. Constitution

All of us want to believe in the freedom of religion, the freedom of speech, the freedom of assembly, and the freedom of petition. The constitution gives us the right to be able to do such things without consequence and, as beings created by the Higher Power, we're able to practice free will. God has given us the ability to choose to act the way we want to act. We're able to make a decision from two or more options or possibilities. But is free will really free? Is it verum?

> *99% think: We always have a choice. We can do anything we want.*

Let's try to analyze how we make decisions in life. We can do that by analyzing this next statement and tackling it piece by piece.

> *Given a particular situation, we make a decision based on what we think is best at that point in time.*

"What we think is best"

'Best' may not be the actual best choice; it's only what we *think* is best. Our decision may be what's best for us, or it may be what's best for others, but we only think of what's best based on what we've learned. A mother may choose to spend money on her child rather than on herself. It seems like a good choice, or the right thing to do, but let's say that the same mother didn't learn that sacrificing for her child is the better option. She didn't learn it from her parents, either because they didn't believe it, or because they weren't around.

We can only choose the best option based on what we have learned; we may learn that the better option is to benefit yourself or we may learn that the better option is to benefit others. We also learn where to spend our money; we may learn to spend money only on essentials, like food and clothes, or we may learn to spend money on luxuries. Either way, the best option is not always the *absolute* best – it's only best from our perspective, based on what we perceive as real. The best option may not even make sense, the best option may not be logical, but we've learned to choose a certain way. It makes sense to us, it's logical to us, but our best is only based on the reality we have created.

"Point in time"

What does this mean? We said earlier that everything we say and do is only learned, but it *is* learned over time. We can only make a decision based on what we've learned by the time the situation is presented to us. We won't choose to become a lawyer, or a nurse, or a housewife, if our logic and priorities don't dictate such when the choice is offered, even if it's something we'd choose later in life. We sometimes look back on previous decisions thinking we should have chosen differently, but we couldn't have made a different choice. We may say that now, having learned more, but we simply didn't have that information or experience in the past.

Our realities change through time as we continue to gather more knowledge and as we learn how to apply the available information. The 'point in time' at which an option is presented dictates the parameters by which we understand our decision.

"Particular situation"

Situations are never the same when we make decisions. We may be presented with options when we're in our clearest mind or our worst condition. We may be preoccupied with something else when we make a choice. We may be stressed. Maybe our child is being annoying, so we just say "Yes". Situations vary, and the parameters of our decisions vary with them. Even decisions made with the same belief system, at the same time in our lives, may prompt different responses if the situation isn't the same.

> *Given a particular situation, we make a decision based on what we think is best at that point in time.*

Combined, these factors form the perfect storm. Our decisions result from a unique outlook filtered through a unique time and situation.

Destiny

Some people believe in destiny. It happens when boy meets girl and they discover that they're soulmates destined to live happily ever after. But we know that this fairy tale never happens. Some people view destiny as a force that makes everything happen, concluding that everything happens for a reason. This means that, no matter what decision we make, the result will still be the same.

Some people don't like the idea of destiny. They want to be in control of their lives; they want the power to change the future. Both are interesting viewpoints, but where is the verum?

1% think: Choice is only an illusion. You can only choose freely once your mind is free from the stress box.

We think we have a choice, but our choices are predetermined. This isn't the same predetermination that we think of when we imagine destiny. In fact, our choice has been predetermined by us. We created a reality in our minds, and within that reality, we can only choose a certain way. We believe that we have options. These options hypothetically exist, but we're unable to choose any but that which we have learned to choose. The other options, even though they are possibilities for a random person, are unavailable to us as individuals. We can only operate according to our pre-determined box. The choice seems real, it feels real, but it isn't verum.

Let's say you go to your favorite restaurant. What do you order? Theoretically, you have maybe two to four main entrées you're choosing from. Despite the fact that there are other choices on the menu, they're not available to you as genuine options. You may not like chicken, so all the chicken entrées are out of the question. You may dislike vegetables, so all the salads are automatically out. What I'm trying to point out is that these options are possible, but not in your mind. They are available in a technical sense, but your mind eliminated them according to your tastes. You've learned to dislike them, or to prefer other options. Either way, you've learned to shut out other options, rendering them unavailable to your mind. You do this because of the concepts that you have in your mind; because you think those concepts are real. And they are! They're as real as the perfect circle, as real as electromagnetic waves, as real as Santa. But what is real, and what is verum?

Summary

There's a particular experiment B.F. Skinner did that's worth mentioning. He placed a rat in the operant chamber and locked it, then delivered an electric shock to the chamber. The rat ran around tirelessly, looking for a way out. After the electric shock, the rat calmed down. Skinner delivered another shock, and the same thing happened. He did it several times. Then, there came a time that Skinner shocked the rat, but the rat wouldn't run anymore. The rat had learned that there was no use running around, because there was no escaping the chamber. Skinner did it a few more times to see if the response would change, but the rat simply stayed. Skinner then opened the door of the chamber, but the rat wouldn't come out. Skinner delivered another shock, and still the rat stayed. Despite the fact that there was now an option to get out, the rat couldn't see it. It had learned that there was no escaping the chamber. The rat perceived this as real: it became as real as the perfect circle, as real as electromagnetic waves, and as real as Santa, and yet, it was only learned.

We can combine what we've learned in these past couple of sections into two words – 'learned reality'. The true origins of our stresses have been fed to us since we were born. We've been blinded to the verum by our creation of a world that's merely real. Once we live in the real world, we cannot see the verum.

As a matter of fact, contained in the past two sections is everything you need to know in order to live the simple and easy life. If you weren't able to completely understand the preceding concepts, I strongly suggest that you reread these sections at a time convenient for you. But for now, let's continue to the pause, during which you can experience these concepts in action.

Exercises

Let's take another week to contemplate what we've discussed. It's a lot to take in. These *are* abnormal ideas, but they're ideas that make sense.

Think about how you perceive certain concepts. Think about your beliefs. Think about your reality. Look back at how you learned these beliefs, these realities, and the world that you live in. Are they real, or are they verum?

Look at your stress box. In Week 1, you had a list of things that stress you out. Go back to that list. See if what I say is verum. See if the only reason it stresses you out is because it's outside the box you created.

Think of your choices, every choice you make. Are you able to really choose other options, or have you learned to choose the one option that you think is best?

Once you're done looking at your learned reality, at the stress box you've created, look at other people's realities, their stress boxes. Start with the person closest to you. It may be your significant other, or your sibling, or your friend or coworker. Look at random people in the mall or at the grocery store. Look at how their realities affect you. Look at how their stress boxes affect you. Look at how their choices affect you. Then vice versa. Look at how you affect them.

The aim of these exercises is to help you see the real versus the verum. Soon, you'll start to see beyond what is real, and start living in the verum.

Pause

Life Should Be Simple and Easy

NOTES

_____

_____

_____

_____

_____

_____

_____

_____

_____

_____

_____

_____

_____

_____

_____

_____

_____

_____

_____

_____

_____

_____

_____

_____

Week 4

The Higher Power

Recap

Another week has gone by. Now, let's review what we know thus far. In Week 1, we addressed being ready and how being ready means being open-minded. I mentioned earlier that this book will challenge many, if not all, of your pre-existing beliefs, and that includes religion. It may take effort to sustain an open mind, so be conscious of maintaining that state as we continue.

In Week 2, we discussed how the past determines today and how we're only a result of what we've learned. Every action, every word, and every thought emerges from our experiences in life. That includes everything you know about religion and the Higher Power.

Finally, in Week 3, we tackled what's real and how things only become real when you grant them that status. At this point, you should be questioning how your own perspective has been shaped by ideas, perceptions, and thoughts from society. Is the religion we know real or verum? Is the Higher Power we know verum?

This Week's Content

A **lot of people shy away** from talking about religion because it's considered sacred. Questioning religion is seen as questioning the Higher Power, rendering the search for truth a sin. Is it any wonder they leave the discussion to the professionals? Perhaps not, but I believe this process of questioning is essential to learning what is verum.

I'm no expert on religion; I'm not a priest or a pastor. In fact, the knowledge of the Christian faith I have is from my father's Catholicism and my mother's faith as a Seventh Day Adventist. I grew up knowing more about the former, in which there are many rules, sacraments, novenas, rosaries, and saints. I was educated in a Jesuit school from elementary until I graduated college, where the curriculum included Theology. All of this meant I discussed religion in a classroom during the week and in a church on Sunday. On special occasions, I would attend service with my mother at the Seventh Day Adventist church, so I had a lot of exposure, but I still cannot say that I'm an expert. In this section, I'll write largely on the Christian faith, but even if you're not Christian, I believe that the following concepts will still help you.

What I do have is the willingness to see the verum in every situation. With the knowledge about religion that I acquired over the years, and the ability to see what is verum, I'm able to decipher the mysteries hidden in our religion. My goal now is not to try and destroy what you know about your religion, but to strengthen your understanding of it. However, in the process, I will tear down the edifice of your faith, then build it back up.

I can tell you right now, with all honesty, that I have seen the Higher Power. Over the course of this week, I'll attempt to show the Higher Power to you, too.

Doubting the Higher Power

> *99% think: Their religion is the true religion and their god is the true god.*

When we think of a Higher Power, what characteristics come to mind? The Higher Power must be all-knowing. The Higher Power must be fair. The Higher Power must be just. But the Higher Power must also be forgiving. The Higher Power must be kind. Would it not be awful if the Higher Power was unfair, unjust, unforgiving, and unkind? Shall we agree that the Higher Power is fair, just, forgiving, and kind? In your mind, you answered "Yes" to that. And you seem to have said "Yes" with some confidence.

Some may say that they've never doubted the Higher Power at all. If we fully believe and trust in our god, we should feel blessed, graced, and at peace. However, one reason you're here today is that you want to change your life, because the life that the Higher Power has given you is not satisfactory. We succumb to the stresses of life because we don't believe in our heart of hearts that this Higher Power will save us. We may have had panic attacks, heartburn, or other bodily manifestations of stress because our faith in our god is not strong, because we have doubted the Higher Power more than once in our life. Because we have seen the Higher Power being seemingly unfair, unjust, unforgiving, and unkind.

Can you see the irony in that? We believe in a religion that we have lived with for years, we have faith in that religion, but we doubt the very essence of our religion – the Higher Power. We will die for our religion, but we doubt our god. It doesn't add up.

There have been so many attempts to prove the existence of this Higher Power, but they have failed. Even scientific research and experimentation were unsuccessful in providing proof of the Higher Power. What makes us so confident that such a being exists? And if it does exist, and we are so certain about it, why do we doubt the Higher

Power? We say one thing, yet we do another. If we believe in our god, we wouldn't be in this place to start with, right?

For now, let's continue and allow our doubt to fester. If we doubt our god, then it must follow that we doubt our religion. We worship in church every single Sunday, and we're somewhat refreshed during the service, but almost immediately after, we go back to our old selves. Life kicks in, and we doubt the god that we thought was real during the Sunday service. We look around at the other people in our service. They say they know our god, they praise our god at all times, the name of our god comes out of their mouths, but they act as if they don't know this god. They, like us, feel stressed because they don't trust that this god is fair, just, forgiving, and kind.

We go to religious retreats, and we feel enlightened and empowered by the grace of God. We feel invincible; able to handle anything that life throws at us. But how long does this last? A day, maybe two or three, at the most. Then, again, we go back to square one, the lost sheep trying to find our way. What seems to be the problem, here? There's a perpetual cycle of highs and lows, but mostly lows. Do we not have faith in our religion? Do we not believe in our god? We talk to priests, pastors, scholars in the field, trying to get a better understanding of our religion, but where does that lead us? More doubt and more anxiety.

Faith in the Higher Power

When we see what is verum, we don't need faith in our religion, and we don't need to believe in our god. These are strong words. What is 'faith', anyway? And what does it mean to 'believe'?

faith
strong belief or trust in someone or something

believe
to accept or regard (something) as true
– Merriam-Webster Dictionary

We then come across more words like 'belief' and 'trust'. What do they really mean?

belief
a feeling of being sure that someone or something exists or that something is true

trust
belief that someone or something is reliable, good, honest, effective, etc.
– Merriam-Webster Dictionary

Life Should Be Simple and Easy

Having faith and believing means that we're attempting to be sure that someone or something exists – that it is verum. Having faith in our religion is accepting that what we hear in church is real and that our Higher Power exists, despite the fact that we have not seen, heard, or touched it. We rely on this information that has been passed on over millennia. Do you really think that information passed down through that many generations didn't change? What we're really doing is blindly believing in someone or something that no person can ever prove is verum. And so we say, "That's why it's called faith."

> *Then Jesus told him, "Because you have seen me,*
> *you have believed; blessed are those who have*
> *not seen and yet have believed."*
> – John 20:29, NIV *Bible*

Earlier, I said that you wouldn't need to have faith, nor would you need to believe. The reason I said this is that you'll be able to *know* your god. You'll be able to see, hear, and touch your god. And when you do, you won't need to have faith or believe, because you'll know. And on that day, you'll never doubt the Higher Power ever again. Does it sound like a fantasy? Does it sound like I'm crazy? I'll let you be the judge.

A God for Everyone

Let's stop doubting your religion and assume that you truly believe, with no room for any doubt. Your religion states that you will be saved if you believe in your god. If you're Christian, then Jesus is the Christ who will save humanity from darkness, and only through Jesus can you attain this salvation. Now, if a person were born in India, to a family that practices Hinduism, this person would not be saved. If a person were born in a communist country like China, where the formation of religious groups is not allowed, this person would not be saved. If a person were born in the Middle East, in a family of Muslims, this person would not be saved. If a person were born in a family of idol worshipers, this person would not be saved. And so on, and so forth.

The Higher Power that we speak of, the one that is fair, and just, and forgiving, and kind, doesn't fit with this idea. Your god has punished these people for not believing in your Christ, but did they choose to be born in a different culture? Does that not manifest an unfair god? One may say that they need to convert to Christianity, as if it were that easy. The same way that we believe in our religion, others believe in theirs. It's as easy for them to simply change their religion (and know they 'need' to do so) as it would be for you to change yours.

If you practice a different religion, the same applies.

So, basically, if your religion is the true religion, then everyone else is doomed. That's what it truly comes down to. You were just lucky enough to be born in this culture and this religion. Or maybe your god made it so, and your god has also made it so that the others are doomed. Where now is the god who is fair? And just? And forgiving? And kind?

Earlier, we agreed that the Higher Power is fair, just, forgiving, and kind. Since this is the case, can we also agree that the Higher Power who will save you will also save the others? The Higher Power won't only save others if they believe in your Christ; the Higher Power will save them despite them believing in another god, because the Higher Power is fair, and just, and forgiving, and kind. The Higher Power doesn't place conditions on its grace. The Higher Power is unconditional.

In Week 3, we tackled what's real. Things only become real once we think they're real, and what we think is only dictated by how society has brought us up. Do you remember Santa Claus? The feeling that you had when you were a kid that Santa was real is the same feeling you have about your religion. No one can convince you otherwise. You have the written scriptures to prove it, just like you had those presents from Santa. Catholics have the flesh and blood of Jesus in their bread and wine, and Santa has milk and cookies. But at some point, someone has to tell you that Santa isn't real, or else you figure it out for yourself.

The concepts above make perfect sense. Otherwise, we're led to believe in a Higher Power that is unjust, unfair, unforgiving, and unkind. Religion is only as real as we think it is; as real as Santa and the concept of the circle. The idea of religion doesn't bear weight or mass, yet it becomes real.

1% think: There is no true religion.

The Sacred Scripture

After tearing down religion, let's start to build it back up. What is the backbone of religion? Every religion is different, but most religions have their own sacred scripture, be it the Bible, the Qur'an, the Torah, or something else. The bottom line is that there is a piece of writing that has been passed on down generations. This piece of writing has been interpreted in many different ways, but until now, scholars, scientists, and religious ministry are still trying to figure out the meaning of the writing. What does it really mean? What is verum?

99% think: The words in the sacred scriptures cannot be broken.

First, we have to understand that there are several types of writing, like newspapers, novels, brochures, blogs, etc., but each type of writing has a specific purpose. History books are meant to document the events of the past, newspapers are meant to document and interpret the present, novels are there to entertain us, brochures or flyers are marketing tools. I could go on, but I think you get the picture. Now, let's try to understand the purpose of religious writing.

Religious writing tries to explain in words the existence of a Higher Power. No one knows for certain who this Higher Power is or the form it truly takes; I've seen the Higher Power, but I can't explain this being through words. To explain it in words is almost impossible, so how is it that these scriptures were written?

Well, partially it's about showing how the Higher Power has worked through people, through situations, and narrating their story to show the reader the works of the Higher Power. Another way is through symbols. Just like in the book of Genesis in the Holy Bible; God didn't create the world in seven days, but this was symbolically written in order to portray the Higher Power's creation of the world and the placement of humankind within it.

The incorrect way to interpret religious writing is to read it literally. When you read a novel, you don't expect it to be real; the events in the novel can certainly happen in real life, but that doesn't make them real. We need to understand that religious writing is created for a certain purpose and that it needs to be read in a certain way. So, it wouldn't be right to dispute the creation of the world by

God in seven days, nor for scientists to try and prove that the scripture is wrong. The scripture isn't right in the sense that the world was created in seven days, but it isn't wrong either, because it wasn't trying to prove that. It was merely giving credit to the Higher Power through a narrative.

Shortly after the creation of the world, the Bible tells of the great flood with which the Higher Power tries to rid the world of sinners. Noah is granted grace and builds an ark, and in the past few decades, maybe even centuries, many have sent expeditions to find this great ark of Noah, all unsuccessful. Similar to creation, the great flood is a narrative with a purpose. Its purpose is to show the reader the power of God and how he has control over life. It also shows how the family of Noah was chosen by God, and that we are symbolic descendants of Noah, in that God also chose us. It can be interpreted in several different ways, but the central idea is that we are governed by a Higher Power, a god who can take life and create life. Therefore, all who remain alive now are chosen by God.

Did you know that the story of Noah isn't an original story? It has actually been dated back to ancient Babylon, as the Sumerian flood myth. It can also be found in the Qur'an, the religious text of Islam. Why is it that this story can be seen at least three different times, in three different religions? This story will probably date back to before writing. It was conceived when men were trying to make sense of the Higher Power. It was then that this story came about, attempting to show the power of God and that this god has chosen you and me to be upon this earth. This story was found to have an impact on people's lives, therefore it was used by neighboring areas, passed on from one generation to another, eventually written down to form the faith of groups that we now call religions.

The first five books of the Bible are called the Pentateuch, consisting of Genesis, Exodus, Leviticus, Numbers, and Deuteronomy. These books give the narrative of ancient history. Specifically, the story of the oppressed and the oppressors, where the Higher Power leads the former out of slavery and gives them certain graces. Why did they decide to choose this story, out of all other possible timelines in ancient history? Because it's an emotional story. It's a story that can change hearts. It's a story of how the improbable was overcome; a story where we can easily see the Higher Power at work, and therefore a story that makes the reader believe there is a god. Most of the details in the story are, in fact, true, but this is also the case in the movie *Titanic*. Some of the details weren't verum, but they were necessary to serve the author's purpose.

The Pentateuch is part of the Bible that Christians follow, but before the Christians used it, this was the Torah that the Jews use in their religion. As we know, Jesus was known as the King of the Jews. After the death of Jesus, Christianity arose as a religion based on the old writings of

Judaism and the new writings from the birth of Jesus. At that time, some people believed in this new religion, and some people continued to live as the original Jews in Judaism.

One religion has evolved into two, but which is the true religion? Is Jesus the true god they say he is? It's a difficult question to answer, but I want you to try to go back into this ancient time. I want you to picture the world in which these people lived. It is in this way that you can discover the answer to such questions.

Ancient History

In this ancient time, people lived with an oppressive ruler. They lived in an era controlled by the people in power. These government leaders did as they wished, while the masses suffered as slaves. In order to contain the people, and to avoid conflict, these leaders used religion; the leaders worked with the high priests, who would tell the people to do as God desired. For, if they disobeyed their god, they would burn in the fires of hell.

There have been many similar instances in history where governments have used religion to conquer lands and countries, to enslave others and establish total control. Beginning with Christopher Columbus in the late fifteenth century, the Spaniards conquered lands in the Americas – half of South America, most of Central America, and much of North America. They even went as far as Asia, conquering the Philippines in the sixteenth century. For centuries, the Spanish ruled their lands. They were oppressive to the people, forced taxes to be paid to their king, and enslaved the natives to do their bidding. They used the Catholic religion to suppress the people. The Spanish made them believe that this was the will of the Higher Power; that the Higher Power favored their rule, and that the only option was to accept an oppressed life through prayer. They had to continue to pray to the Higher Power and accept suffering, the same way Jesus had.

This god was a punishing god. This god was a being that would send you to hell if you didn't follow his will. The priests told stories of a better place, a heaven; a place up in the clouds, where angels sang and children played all day. You would be able to go there only if you followed God's will. It would be easy to follow God's will if life was easy, wouldn't it? But if you're in a situation where you're oppressed, abused, and forced into labor, it would be so easy to fall into sin.

In the ancient times, the priests would even say that babies were born blind because of the sins of the parents. Because of this, they had to live in shame for the rest of their lives. Lepers were condemned, their illness seen as a punishment from God. They had to atone for their sins for life.

The Christ

It was in this ancient era that Jesus was born. It was a difficult period, but this person knew the verum. He wanted to stand up to these oppressors, but he also knew that he wouldn't stand a chance. Guess what he did? He took a band of Merry Men and started to show people the light. He tried to show the light that doesn't bear mass or weight, but he couldn't say it directly, or they would have beheaded him on the spot for blasphemy. So, he did it through symbols and parables.

When people started seeing this light, they knew that this person was given grace. At that time, such a person was the anointed one, or what they called the 'Christ'. Jesus continued for three years until the high priests finally decided to put an end to his teachings. They weren't happy that people were starting to doubt their religion – it was a challenge to their power and their grip on the masses.

Even the way they wrote the story of Jesus in the Bible was special. They had to write it in a way that people would believe, in which they would still see he was not an ordinary person. He was the one that brings the message of the light; the same light I show you now. The light that doesn't bear mass or weight. Jesus showed the truth or the verum and the light. He is the Christ – Jesus Christ.

Summary

At this point, some people already see what is real and what is verum; the reality in religion, the reason why religion is created, the purpose of the scriptures. In the previous sections, we discussed learned reality. One reality that we learn is the reality of religion and the Higher Power.

Religion is one of our strongest beliefs. My goal in this section isn't to make you a non-believer. I only wish to show you how your religion was created so that the verum of the Higher Power will reveal itself. Once you see the Higher Power, you won't need to have faith, because now you *know*.

Exercises

As in the previous weeks, I'd like to leave you with a task. I'd like you to start contemplating your religion. Think about how it was formed. Think about the verum behind your religion, the writings, the rituals. But before that, I'd like you to analyze another religion, the religion of idol worshipers. It's a simple and primitive religion; we don't need experts to be able to analyze this religion, but we do need common sense (and the tools from the previous weeks) to see the verum behind the religion, how it was formed, and the reason it was invented.

Idol worshipers weren't only present in primitive times; they also existed a few centuries ago in isolated groups that hadn't had access to other religions. Some of these groups used inanimate objects like the sun or the mountains. Some carved man-like figures on stones to worship. Some used living creatures, like elephants, bears, lions, monkeys, and even plants and trees.

Think of why they used these objects to worship. Is it their fault that they didn't know the god that you know? Were they wrong, in worshiping these objects? Also, think of how they passed their worship from generation to generation. Think of the stories they told their children, then think of the similarities to your own religion. Think of how it was created, how it was passed on, and find the why in all this. Be open, and look for what is verum.

For some people, the realization might be instantaneous. For some, it may take days or weeks, so take your time. Do it at your own pace. Feel free to read this section again, so that you may understand it better, and remember that I only offer the verum, nothing else.

Pause

Life Should Be Simple and Easy

NOTES

_____

_____

_____

_____

_____

_____

_____

_____

_____

_____

_____

_____

_____

_____

_____

_____

_____

_____

_____

_____

_____

_____

_____

_____

Week 5

Today Does Not Rely on the Past

Recap

I t's been a month now, since we first started. I understand that the journey is long. The exercises you've done after each week have, I hope, proven the necessity of that.

Initially, we went into the state of fractus to prepare us to hear the truth – the verum that the 1% see and know. We then continued to discuss how we were created and the origin of our stresses – our learned realities. We started to see what is real versus what is verum. We now know that things only become real if we think of them as such; as real as the perfect circle and as real as Santa. One heavy example we tackled was that of religion. If we're able to see the verum in a belief as strong and as deep-seated as a religion, this will hopefully lead us to question every belief we have.

This knowledge, when applied, will propel you towards the De Novo event – the awakening to a new life. This section will show you how to apply your newfound knowledge in this way.

This Week's Content

Everything **is predetermined,** but we've already established that it's predetermined by you. You have created your own reality in accordance with what you think is real and not what is verum, but you can change all that. You can be in control of your actions. You can create your own destiny as you see fit, not dictated by what you've learned.

Responsibility

Before you take that leap, you need to realize that the world we live in has systems and we still need to follow them. If we didn't have these systems, everyone would run amok and chaos would ensue. It's your constitutional right to use any information in this book to achieve the life that you seek, but know that you're still responsible for your actions and their outcomes, whether positive or negative.

Life Should Be Simple and Easy

Is it Wrong?

Clasp your hands together as if you were praying, then look at the illustration below. See whether your right thumb is over your left or vice versa.

Now, try to do it the other way. If your left thumb is over the right, do it the other way. How does it feel? It feels awkward, doesn't it? It doesn't feel right. Actually, it feels wrong. But, *is* it wrong? Let me explain what wrong is, by defining what's right.

> **right**
> *morally or socially correct or acceptable*
> – Merriam-Webster Dictionary

Being right is being socially correct or acceptable. This means that in order to be right, something has to be accepted by society; it has to agree with the 99%. If we're doing what the 1% does, we'll go against society. We won't be normal. We will be socially incorrect and, therefore, we'll be wrong. In fact, not just wrong, but abnormal. And what do they call abnormal people? Crazy. We will be crazy wrong. But is that really wrong?

Even if it isn't, that's how it feels. This feeling is the reason we're unable to choose the other options, because these options feel wrong. We've learned to think in a certain way, and we therefore act in a certain way. Our actions are predictable, because we only do things one way, and it's the one way that feels right. The options that feel right are the options that fit in the box – your stress box.

Preservation of the Ego

Why is it difficult to look outside the box? The natural human action is to preserve the self or the ego. We must not hurt ourselves, and when we try to do something that feels wrong, our ego is hurt. We try to revert to the comfortable, to where it's safe. This is what makes us stay where we are. We've built a whole world of reality, and we've lived with that reality for however long we've been alive. We've poured our sweat and blood into it, spent a lifetime building it; this is where we feel comfortable. This is where we feel safe.

What I'm trying to do is to bring down that reality. To see the verum, we need to demolish the stress box. The only reason it's difficult to go outside the box is the fact that it feels awkward. But is it wrong?

The reason we feel stressed is that our ego is hurt. Our ego is trying to keep itself safe by maintaining our constructed reality. If we're unable to conform with the 99%, we won't be normal. We'll be abnormal, and our ego won't allow it. Our ego will make sure we're comfortable, it will keep us safe, but in order to find what's verum, we'll need to go against our egos and even ourselves. It *will* feel awkward, it won't feel right, but is it wrong?

Opinions

One of the reasons our egos don't want to go outside the box is the opinions of others. You may have figured out what opinions actually are, by now, but for those who haven't, let me explain a little further.

Opinions are based on beliefs, and what did we say about beliefs? Beliefs are only learned; people act and react based on their reality. The same way that you've learned your reality, other people have learned theirs. Their opinions, therefore, are only based on that learned reality. Their opinions of you are real, and a poor opinion hurts. This pain is based on your perception of real as well as the other person's perception of real, but it is not verum.

When other people's opinions fit in our reality, we actually like it. When other people commend us for what we do, we feel positive about it. But when people don't accept, or do not condone, our actions, our egos get hurt. But it doesn't *have* to hurt. When we see the verum, we don't need to hurt.

Why do their opinions have to fit our reality? Your reality is totally different from another person's; even twins have different realities. Since no one has the exact same reality, the possibility of having your reality be the same as someone else's is almost impossible. In trying to fit into someone else's reality, we're trying to do the impossible. So, why keep trying?

Consequences

Another reason we fear leaving our stress box is the possible consequences of such action. We may fear unfamiliar experiences or results that will feel wrong. We have been conditioned to believe that making mistakes will bring about negative consequences. We go through school, graded according to tests and exams. The fewer mistakes we make, the higher our score. Competitive games, like sports, have a winner and a loser, and everyone wants to be the winner. The winner gets a trophy, recognition, and other rewards for being the best. Losing isn't an option; there is no reward for losing.

Making mistakes will be outside the stress box. Making mistakes will feel wrong. Therefore, we're afraid to make mistakes, because negative consequences are outside the box.

> *Learn from the mistakes of others. You can never live long enough to make them all yourself.*
> – Groucho Marx

We've all heard this quote, and it makes perfect sense. Despite that, we still insist on making mistakes. Why do I say that? All of us have been told by our parents not to do certain things. It's through their experiences that they obtained the knowledge of which actions lead to negative consequences. They've already made the mistake for us to learn from. Yet, what did we do? We still did it, didn't we? Then we realized, in the end, that it really was a mistake.

Our first instinct isn't to learn from other people's mistakes, because life isn't learned that way. We learn through experience. Experience leads to true learning. So, don't hold back because of your fear of negative consequences.

I'll tell you now that the consequences of thinking like the 1% are positive, but I know you won't listen, because you have fears – fear of negative consequences and fear of other people's opinions. These fears are real; as real as the concept of the circle, as real as Santa. But are they verum?

Make the Pain Go Away

The life that you seek is simple and easy, but the path towards it is difficult, arduous, and grueling. For people who are willing to make the jump, pain awaits. It hurts to go outside the box. It feels awkward. It doesn't feel right. But is it wrong?

The further you step outside the box, the more painful it will be. Know, though, that the feeling of pain is only as real as we make it. You can start with baby steps. Start with something simple, then progress towards something further and further outside the box. One day, you'll realize that there is no box. You'll realize that the stress box is only a creation of your mind. Our authors suffered through the same painful process, as Conrad shares:

"Without going into too much detail, let me tell you my painful story. My story is not too different from yours. I had over 30 years to create my stress box. I suffered through the same stresses you're feeling, and I too wanted a way out.

"I grew up in a family with rules. Ours probably had a few more than most. Some of these rules were traditions and some were religious. These rules were instilled in me by my parents and were reinforced by my relatives – my grandparents, aunts, uncles, cousins, and siblings. My parents wanted the best for me, and they tried to get it the way they knew best, by enforcing rules."

> *Sticks and stones may break my bones, but words will never hurt me.*
> – Proverb

"My parents didn't hit me, but they sure had a way of letting me know when I broke the rules. They scolded me in front of my siblings, and occasionally in front of my other relatives. I felt embarrassed and humiliated. If that wasn't enough, they told me how incompetent I was as a person. They showed me how I was wrong by man and how I was wrong by God. I still remember my grandparents citing the fifth commandment – you should honor your father and mother.

"At the end of the day, I didn't have any broken bones, but the same words that some say can't hurt ended up shaping my reality. Broken bones can heal, but what's in my mind will be there forever. I lived through their words for the longest time. I felt alone.

"I went to med school, where I experienced a stress-induced heart attack at the age of 23. At that time, I wasn't ready to live the simple and easy life. I got married shortly after med school. My family didn't approve of my wife, and we moved into a home far away from them. But my family continued to show their presence, and their rules and the resultant reality certainly didn't leave me. Even then, I wasn't ready.

"We got pregnant, and my wife carried the pregnancy for nine months with no complications. Hours into labor, the doctor couldn't find the baby's heartbeat. We had a stillbirth. It wasn't easy coming home to an empty crib, and I turned to my family for support, only to hear how I was wrong by man and even more wrong by God. You might think this is the point where I went into fractus, but not quite yet.

"I was presented with an opportunity that took me around the globe and far, far away from my family, but it meant being away from my wife and my one-year-old son. I figured that if I went as far away as possible from my family, I would be free of their rules, free of my reality, and therefore free of stress. It was the obvious choice, so I took it.

"At that time, I was both figuratively and literally alone. Being alone gave me time to think about my situation. All my stresses started to come out into the open, one by one. I started to have panic attacks in the middle of nowhere; I'd be buying groceries or driving and experience severe anxiety. I couldn't understand why I couldn't achieve the life I wanted. I did my best, I tried ways to decrease my stress, but where did it leave me? I was even more stressed than before.

"I didn't want an extravagant lifestyle. I didn't want a

high-paying job. I didn't even want a large house or new car; all I wanted was a simple life. I wanted a place we could call home, to be with my wife and son, and to live life happily ever after. Why could my god not give me this simple life?

"I did my utmost to follow the rules. I wasn't a murderer or thief, I didn't try to take advantage of people, so why did my god grant everyone else a better life but me? My neighbors had a better life, my relatives had a better life, so why didn't I?

"If God was fair, then I should at least have a good life, right? But I didn't. Therefore, God was not fair. But is there a god that's not fair? No, it's impossible, so the only possible explanation was that God didn't exist. I gave up on life, and I gave up on God. *This* made me ready.

"It's said that when the student is ready, the teacher will come, but the path to this life wasn't shown to me the way that I have mapped it out for you. I had several teachers giving me different pieces of information. It took a lot of figuring out, but I did have one mentor who guided me through the process.

"I was as skeptical as you; despite the fact that the information made sense, I still didn't want to believe. The information was logical and made perfect sense, but because it was outside my reality, I couldn't believe it. I couldn't abandon my reality. The rules that were set by my family, religion, culture, and society bound me tightly.

"I struggled with this for weeks and months. I said it straight to my mentor's face, "What you're telling me isn't right." But he knew it wasn't right because it didn't feel right to *me*. It felt awkward, and it felt wrong. It was unfamiliar territory, and I was fearful.

"Every time I stepped out of my reality, it hurt. My mind was fighting it. I wanted to stay where it felt comfortable, in my old disappointing life. I wanted to stay safe. I loved my reality. I didn't want to let it go. Even though I had so much stress in that life, I wanted to be there for all eternity. Even though it made sense to leave my disappointing life for one that was better, it was still easier for me to stay and be stressed than get out and feel uncomfortable and unsafe. Because, at that time, I was comfortably stressed.

"But something in me kept pushing forward. My heart was sick and tired of my old life. The verum in me wanted to get out. My heart couldn't accept this disappointing life any longer. My heart wouldn't accept that there was a simple and easy life out there that I couldn't reach.

"Boom! I experienced my De Novo event. I still remember that day as if it were yesterday. Nothing heavy dragging me down anymore. I could tell, in that instant, that from that day onward, life wouldn't be the same. I can see the verum, now; the true way of things.

"So, I tried to get out of my reality. I started to break the rules, and it hurt. I started to challenge religion, sway from societal norms, and say "No" to family, and it hurt more. I tried a little bit more, and it hurt a little bit more. But, believe it or not, it yielded different results – results that Einstein defined as not insane, because I did something different. The decisions I made were outside my reality, and so were the consequences. Choosing a different option hurt, and yes, there were times that the consequences hurt. Some of the consequences were positive, and sometimes they weren't what I'd hoped for. I experimented ceaselessly, but the more mistakes I made, the more I learned. I was starting to live in the verum, but I could still feel the pain. It took me months.

"It was difficult to trust the verum, because the results seemed disastrous, at times. I didn't have much experience with the verum, but as it produced more positive experiences, I learned to trust it more and more. I challenged religion, and it hurt me, probably the same way that it hurt you. But then, the Higher Power revealed itself in a way I couldn't even fathom.

"Even months after my De Novo event, I still felt the pain when I left my stress box. It wasn't the same pain I had felt before, though. Now, I could identify the pain as a feeling of being uncomfortable and unsafe. Now, I know that this pain is not verum, and being uncomfortable is so much better than being stressed.

"I tried to do things that weren't normally accepted by society, and it hurt. I tried to do things that weren't normally accepted by me, and it hurt even more. It could be as simple as choosing something else at McDonald's, or it could be going against some of my compulsions to be perfect. I learned that, a lot of the time, good enough is good enough.

"Whenever I encounter a situation, I try to see what's real and what's verum. Sometimes, it's difficult to see what's verum, especially in circumstances that are stressful. It takes me a while to realize the verum, but I do. Some situations take more time and effort than others, and there are times when I want to choose what's real over what's verum. Force of habit kicks in. These are the times that I want to go back to my old, disappointing life, because it feels safe. It's difficult to destroy a whole world that took 30 years to build, and there have been times that I chose the real, only to realize that it's still the wrong choice. So, I continue to learn.

"Over time, situations became easier to read. I can see the verum with less time and effort and, once I do, I get to choose freely. When you see the verum, everything becomes clear. Everything makes sense. But even now, I still get into sudden situations where I'm unable to see the verum fast enough to make a decision. So, I still choose the real. I still have parts of my reality in my mind. It hasn't completely gone away, and maybe it never will. But this is now my 1%. 1% of the time, I think like the 99%, and 99% of the time, I think like the 1%. So, the pain never goes away. It will always be there. The only difference is that now, I know that it's only as real as I make it. Now, I only experience stress for a few seconds every year. I wouldn't trade that for anything in the world."

Summary

The battle now is within yourself. My only goal is to provide you with the information and knowledge that you need to win, but I cannot fight this battle for you. This is the very reason you need to be ready. If you don't have the heart to go on, to fight back against your ego, you will simply stay where you are.

Most self-help books claim they'll inspire you to change yourself, because in changing, you may achieve something better. But I don't want you to change, because change is difficult. All I want you to do is to see the verum and to act on it. The moment you knew that Santa wasn't real, did you need to change? Again, I only offer the verum. The rest is up to you.

Life Should Be Simple and Easy

Exercises

Find out how it feels to be wrong. Try to clasp your hands again, then do it the other way. Think of your routines. Think of the sequence of tasks you do when you wake up in the morning. What do you do first? What do you do next? Think of the way you take a shower. What do you wash first? What comes next? Try to do it in a different order. How does it feel? This is how it feels when you start going outside your stress box. It will feel awkward. It won't feel right. But is it wrong?

Everything is learned. Thus far, I've been asking you to observe your actions and the actions of others. You've been examining how these actions come about and how they tie into each other. But now, it's time to get up from where you are and do something with your life.

Experience is the best teacher, and mistakes are the best lessons.
– Anonymous

Life's lessons, especially, are learned through experience. Life's lessons are learned by living. If you so choose, now is the time to destroy the reality that you've loved all your life. It's time to let go. The ball is in your court, now. All you have to do is jump.

Pause

NOTES

_____

_____

_____

_____

_____

_____

_____

_____

_____

_____

_____

_____

_____

_____

_____

_____

_____

_____

_____

_____

_____

_____

_____

_____

_____

_____

Life Should Be Simple and Easy

Week 6

Life Should Be Simple and Easy

Recap

By now, you may be on the path to the life that's simple and easy. If you're doing it hard, you're doing it wrong. The difficult way to have a better life is to make major changes, changing your thoughts or even the way you think. But the purpose of this book is not to change your life, nor is it to change the way you think. The only goal of this book is to show you what is verum, so that you're able to determine what's real and what's verum. Nothing else.

All the previous sections have brought us to this final step. In Week 1, we realized how life was broken and accepted that all our actions were in vain. This led us to a point of fractus where we opened our minds to the truth – the verum.

In Weeks 2 and 3, we discussed how powerful our minds are in creating real worlds. These learned realities are built from childhood and predetermine our actions, behaviors, and stresses. We then learnt what is real and what is verum.

By tackling religion as a firmly established belief in Week 4, we were able to learn how our other beliefs seem real versus the verum.

In Week 5, we found out that living in the verum feels awkward, but it isn't necessarily wrong. The pain of leaving what's real and living in the verum is only as real as we make it. But as we continue to make steps towards the verum, we will soon achieve our De Novo event – the awakening to a new life.

This Week's Content

Once you're able to see the verum, you'll be able to attain the life you seek. In this week, I will only be providing you with questions. These questions are meant for you to better examine the verum of life. Please take your time thinking about these questions and answering them to the best of your abilities.

Me, Myself, and I

Over these past five weeks, you've examined yourself thoroughly. Have you found the verum version of yourself? Let's start with your past. Worrying about your past robs you of today. So, let's face your past and find the verum.

- How did you learn to do what you do?
- Who taught you what you know?
- You made decisions you're not proud of, but how did those decisions come about?

- Were you able to choose freely, or were those decisions predetermined by what you'd learned?
- Were they only the best choice given the knowledge that you had and the situation at that particular point in time?
- Were those decisions only directed by your reality – a reality that was not verum?
- Could you have chosen another option at that time?
- If you think you didn't have a choice, then why blame yourself for what you've done?
- Why torture yourself for your past?
- The better question is, have you sinned against your Higher Power because of these decisions?
- Does the all-knowing Higher Power not know what is verum?

Let's continue to examine the consequences of your past, present, and future. Your past decisions may have led to negative consequences, some of which you could still be dealing with today.

- Why did you label certain things as negative consequences?
- Think about a person born into poverty, maybe even a person born in a third-world country. Is it wrong to be poor?
- Why do you think that it's wrong to be poor?

- How did you learn that it's wrong to be poor?
- Does your Higher Power discriminate against poor people?
- Does your Higher Power not love poor people?
- Are you afraid to be poor?
- Why are you afraid to be poor?
- What's wrong with being poor?
- Is it just wrong because it's outside your reality?
- Now, think of other possible consequences. Is it wrong to be in jail?
- Is it wrong to live with your parents?
- Is it wrong that your loved one has left you?
- Why does it feel wrong?

So many possible consequences are out there. Yes, you may have made decisions that created these outcomes, and you may make future decisions that create these outcomes.

- But is it wrong?
- Does the Higher Power discriminate against you for causing such consequences?
- Does the Higher Power not know the verum?

Know your past and own it. Once you see the verum in your past, you'll know the verum of today – how you've learned to be who you are. Your past shouldn't continue to haunt you. You know that if it does, it's only a part of your old reality, and not what's verum.

The verum will also unlock your future. You'll be able to control the future in the manner you wish. You'll be free of predetermination, knowing that other options are available for you to choose and other outcomes are possible. It may hurt to go outside the real, but know that it is not verum.

The Power of Others

For these past five weeks, you have also been observing other people – their actions, how they learned, and how they affect you. Have you found the verum in others?

- If you think that you've got no choice in your decisions, what makes you think that other people have choices in theirs?
- Do they not operate like you?
- Why, then, blame them for their actions?
- Other people will also include the people who taught you your life. Were they wrong in teaching you what you know?
- Does your Higher Power take note of other people's sins?
- Or does your Higher Power know the verum?

- When other people hurt you, why does it hurt? Why does it feel wrong?
- Other people's actions have consequences for you. Are these consequences wrong?
- Will your Higher Power fault them for causing such consequences?
- Will your Higher Power fault you for living with their consequences?
- What is the only way you can make their realities similar to yours?
- If it took them years to build their reality, what makes you think they can easily change for you?
- Why do the impossible?

See the verum in others the same way you see the verum in you. When you start seeing it, you'll no longer be affected by anyone else.

Coping with Stress

In Week 1, we enumerated several ways of how to cope with stress. Let's review them, now, and search for the verum.

One of them is rationalization. You try to rationalize that you're in a place that's better than most.

- But is it really better? Or is it worse?

- Who says it's better or worse?
- Is this perspective real or verum?
- When you see the verum in your current situation, is it wrong to be in that situation?

Thinking positive is somewhat the same: trying to see the better in your situation.

- Is your situation really so negative that you have to think positive?
- Who says it is negative? Or positive?
- What is verum?

Thinking positive only emphasizes the negative. When you see the verum, you'll know that the negatives only feel wrong because they're outside your stress box. Be content with what you have.

- Why aren't you content in the first place?
- Who says that you need to have more?
- How did you learn to need more than what you have?
- Is that need to have more real or verum?
- Will someone judge you when you have less?
- Or will you judge yourself?
- Whose reality are we talking about, here?
- Who says you have less?

- Is it the poor person who was born in a third-world country who cannot provide?
- Will your Higher Power love you less when you have less?

How about trying not to sweat the small stuff?

- What *is* the small stuff?
- Is it the small stuff that's outside your reality?
- Either big or small, if it's outside your stress box, doesn't it hurt the same way?
- Can you see your stress box?
- Do you see how the root of all stress is your stress box – your reality?

The sooner you see the verum, the sooner you dismantle that box.

- 'Take it one day at a time.' Can't you handle the stress, all at once?
- 'Use distraction to mask the stress.' Why even distract yourself, when there is no stress?
- 'A little bit of stress is important in your life.' Says who?
- Is this real or verum?

Once you've seen the verum, there's no going back.

Summary

Once **you start living this life,** you'll find that there's no need for stress, because your stress box doesn't exist anymore. It may appear every once in a while, but 99% of the time, it's not there.

Everything Else Is Simple and Easy

You may still find some tasks difficult. An example is mathematics and English. People who are good in math have some degree of difficulty with English, and vice versa, but it doesn't have to be this way. The same way that these people who are good at math have learned it, people who are bad at math can learn it, given the proper time and effort.

In Week 2, we talked about how we learn, and one way we do it is through time and effort. You first master the basics, then progress through the rest. Yet, some say that it's still hard to do so. Interest in math, or any subject, does play a factor in that. A person with passion or genuine interest in a certain subject will learn faster. You may need to find that interest in you. It could be the interest in the result, or the interest in the process. The series of books for dummies are a good starting point. The publisher and authors of these books know the process of learning and make it easy. As of the publication of this book, I'm not paid in any way to endorse these books. This is just to let you know that there are ways to achieve other things the simple and easy way.

Personally, I'm good at math. Naturally, I'm bad at English. I flunked my English class in junior year of high school. I have difficulty writing essays and pulling out words from nowhere; it's especially difficult to find words for abstract thoughts, such as the concepts in this book. Yet, here we are. Even though it's a short book, my passion for relaying this message to you was strong enough. After all, we wanted to keep the book simple and easy; if I couldn't accept that the Higher Power would limit this life to the 1%, I needed to make it as accessible as possible. One person who wanted to convey the same message said that he was the way, the verum, and the life. I'm hoping that through this way, you may see the verum and live the life that was meant to be.

Allegory of the Cave

I'll part with an old story. Plato was one of the oldest documented people of the 1%. He saw the verum and, in one of his dialogues, he writes a story of people in a cave. In this story, people were forced into a cave from childhood. They were chained at the end of the cave so that they couldn't move or see the entrance. The cave was dark, but behind them was a fire, which they couldn't see. They could, however, see the shadows in front of them, made by the fire behind. Outside the cave, other people walked by, never coming in. The people inside the cave could only hear them from afar.

They lived like this for a long, long time, until one day, one of them was unshackled and allowed to see the fire. The very first time the person saw the fire, his eyes hurt. It took a while for his eyes to adapt to the light of the fire. At that moment, he saw a new reality; a reality outside the realm of shadows.

The person continued towards the opening of the cave. As he went outside, he was blinded by the light of the sun. Again, it took a while for his eyes to adjust to this new light. Then, he saw a whole new world, a world of other people and lands. He experienced a new reality. He saw this as a far better world than the one in which he'd previously lived.

Should that person go back to the other people in the

cave, he would tell them the story of this new world. The others would see his story as ridiculous, to the extent that if anyone tried to force them out of the cave, they would kill that person.

Plato's allegory has been interpreted many different ways. But for today, it will serve the purpose of showing you the verum and how people interpret the verum. Now, I pray that you may see the light.

Exercises

This will be our final pause. I know the book feels incomplete. I know that there are still a lot of questions running through your mind, right know. Unfortunately, I won't answer these questions. Earlier in this process, I claimed that you'd be able to answer some of life's questions, like, "What's the purpose of life?" Now, I will intentionally not help you out. I know the answers to your questions, but I won't provide them. I said that *you* would be able to answer these questions, not me, because all the information you need to answer these questions has already been given to you. The purpose of this book was to show you the way and give you the tools to find this life that's simple and easy. The only thing left for you to do is to live.

Godspeed on your journey.

Continue your journey at
stress**free**initiative**.org**

Life Should Be Simple and Easy

NOTES

_____

_____

_____

_____

_____

_____

_____

_____

_____

_____

_____

_____

_____

_____

_____

_____

_____

_____

_____

_____

_____

_____

_____

_____

Nonprofit

stress**free**initiative**.org**

This book, on its own, should be sufficient to direct you to the life that's simple and easy. The tools in the book will help achieve this life. But for some, this might not be enough.

We're here to help and here's a short story to illustrate how we do it. There was a man walking on the street and fell into a deep hole with walls too steep to climb. He cried for help, and no one would come. Then, a doctor passed by. The man called for help. The doctor wrote a prescription, threw it down the hole and went along his way. Then, a priest walked by. The man asked for help. The priest wrote a prayer, threw it down the hole and went along his way. Then, a friend passed by. The man begged for help, and without batting an eye, the friend jumped into the hole. The man exclaimed, "Are you crazy?! Now we're both stuck!" The friend calmly said, "Don't worry. I've been in this hole before, and I know how to get out."

Stress Free Initiative is a 501(c)(3) nonprofit

organization that is here to help people like you. People working for the organization have been where you are and are now more than happy to help you get out.

The mission is to help people suffering from depression, anxiety, and stress by bridging the knowledge gap, through self-discovery, on what stress is and how to manage it effectively, as you have seen in this book. We believe that everyone deserves to live a stress-free life, and we're committed to providing the resources and support needed to make that happen.

We're also building a community of people who want to continue their journey with us – a place where we can create a healthy environment for people to share and open up. We welcome all people who have experienced stress in one way or another, regardless of gender, race, religion, or political affiliation, no matter which stage of the journey you're in – from pre-fractus to those who have undergone the De Novo event. It's going to be a community dedicated to helping people achieve the same goal.

The purchase of this book has started to help others. You can continue to pay it forward by donating to the nonprofit. Your donation has the power to transform lives, break stigma, and provide much-needed support to those facing mental health and stressful challenges. Every contribution, no matter the size, will surely help another life. We believe that it should never be necessary to resort to self-inflicted harm, as every life deserves a chance for healing and happiness.

If you can spare some of your time to aid in the cause, we welcome volunteers as well. Hope to see you soon!

Continue your journey at
stress**free**initiative**.org**

Works Cited

Bibliography

Carnegie, Dale. *How to Stop Worrying and Start Living*. New York: Simon & Schuster, 1948.

Watson, John B. *Behaviorism*. New York: W.W. Norton & Company, Inc., 1925.

Merriam Webster's Collegiate Dictionary. Springfield: Merriam-Webster, 2014.

Stevenson, Angus, and Christine A. Lindberg, eds. *New Oxford American Dictionary*. Oxford: Oxford University Press, 2013.

Fishburne, Laurence. *The Matrix*. Directed by Lana Wachowski, and Lilly Wachowski. Burbank, CA: Warner Home Video, 1999.

"File:Operant Conditioning Diagram Rev.Svg - Wikimedia Commons". *Commons.wikimedia.org*. N.p., 2017. Web. 8 Apr. 2017.

"File:BW EM Spectrum.Png - Wikimedia Commons". *Commons.wikimedia.org*. N.p., 2017. Web. 8 Apr. 2017.

The Holy Bible, New International Version. Grand Rapids: Zondervan Publishing House, 1984.

Life Should Be Simple and Easy

About the Authors

Dr. Conrad Aquino, MD

Conrad Aquino, MD sought a career in healthcare. He worked as a physician for several years. At the time of publication, he's Assistant Director of Professional Services for one of the fastest growing healthcare companies in the Washington DC area. He faced many challenges growing up, which continued throughout medical school. At a young age, he experienced a stress-related heart attack, and later, shortly after marriage, chose to uproot himself from his hometown and family to pursue a better life. Unfortunately, life became even more stressful for this doctor, but several anxiety attacks later, Conrad experienced his De Novo event in March of 2008 and has been stress-free ever since.

Bryson Miller

Bryson Miller served as an Aerospace Physiologist in the U.S. Air Force and has a second-degree black belt in kung fu. He joined the military to sustain a relationship and to build a better life, but found that it caused a strain over time. After serving the military, he returned home to be in the comfort of family and friends, unknowing of the challenges that laid waiting: his father was diagnosed with brain cancer, and several of his friends having tragic, untimely deaths. Pressing forward, he continued to try to have a serious relationship, only to find himself in a constant cycle of love and loss. Stress continued to build and pushed him into despair, but Bryson experienced his De Novo event in October of 2010 and has been stress-free ever since.

Made in the USA
Columbia, SC
11 February 2024